NELSON EDDY
AMERICA'S FAVORITE BARITONE

AN AUTHORIZED BIOGRAPHICAL TRIBUTE

By GAIL LULAY

A poignant look at the life of
Nelson Eddy; concert stage, movie,
and radio star - he thrilled millions with
his robust baritone and handsome blond physique.

Gale Sherwood voiced the sentiments of millions when she told "Variety" after Nelson's death, "It's a terrible loss to everyone who ever heard a beautiful voice, saw a wonderful man or knew a kind soul."

Published by Goldfleet Publishing
47 South Milwaukee Avenue
Wheeling, Illinois 60090

ISBN 0-9633336-9-0

Printed in United States of America
FIRST EDITION
First Printing 1992
Front Jacket Photo Courtesy of William & Robert Rush
Designed by Arthur Hackin

DEDICATION

With love and gratitude to my children Catherine and Michael, their spouses Brett and Kiley, my grandchildren Rachel, Alyssa and Jenna who shall know good music, my associates Barbara Rhoads and Colleen Gray for their tireless efforts, and my wonderful family for their love and support.

ACKNOWLEDGEMENTS

From emotions, to ideas, into print; my heartfelt thanks and appreciation to all of Nelson's family. They entrusted me with his life and allowed me to reveal him as he truly was. They shared their most private, though sometimes difficult, emotions and feelings with me so that I might set the record straight.

Nelson's stepson Sidney and his wife Janine; Virginia Brown, Nelson's half sister and her family; Gale Sherwood, his night club partner and her husband Charles Francis; and Thelma Cohen, Nelson's fan club President and her husband Ben; all have given unselfishly of their time and effort on Nelson's behalf.

It is very difficult to write the intimacies necessary for a biography when so few people are alive and memories have long ago faded away. Yet, when I entered the realm of Nelson's life, arms opened and enveloped me with the sharing of memories, anecdotes and photos. What you read is really written memories of those closest to him. My primary sources were The Eddy Association materials, the families' private scrapbooks, diaries and photo albums, and memorabilia such as programs, awards and citations. I supplemented my information with fan publications, movie magazines and other resources which are too old and scattered to document properly. I always verified the information against living sources whenever possible. One of the hardest jobs was researching the information from the Archives of the Performing Arts at the University of California. Nelson's family was a tremendous help in sorting out the accurate versions of the many newspaper articles and various clippings.

My gracious thanks to Elinor Warren Griffin, Robert Armbruster, Susanna Foster, June Haver, Fred MacMurray, Jimmy Stewart, Bob Hope, Alice Faye, Bill and Bob Rush, Kathyrn Grayson, Tom Cooper, Norma Daniels, Lucy and Perry Pickering, Irene Daligga and David Goldstein for their availability and openness regarding Nelson's life.

Also to Ned Comstock and Ann Schlosser at the Archives of the Performing Arts, University of California and Debra Smith of Occidental College in Los Angeles, California. A special thanks to Barbara Butler for remembering; James Ziganto for his assistance in photographing the pictures; Bobbie Rhoads and Colleen Gray for two years of neverending patience and humor; and Art Hackin, my agent for guiding me all the way home.

PREFACE

My eighty-seven year old mother admitted her life-long love affair with Nelson Eddy with typical aplomb; "That voice, those eyes, that hair and my dear....he was <u>such</u> a good and decent gentleman!" Well, there you have it! He possessed a mystique that pulled millions of women to him. Ask any woman over sixty, and these gracious and proper grandmothers will admit that, in their youth, they were impassioned, inspired, and yes, even in love with this blond Adonis.

But the words most often used to describe Nelson Eddy by all who knew him relate directly to his character, not just to his great talent. Words such as righteous, genuine, decent and generous.

Nelson Eddy---the motion picture idol, radio personality, renowned concert singer---could fill an auditorium to overflowing with his beautiful lyric baritone. Though no actor, he was able to project an intimacy through his screen image that touched our hearts. He possessed a rare sense of timing and a pantomimic talent that any comedian would die for! He was a storyteller, a charismatic entertainer. Multi-talented, he was a painter, sculptor and linguist. He could weave a mesmeric hold over any audience he personally touched. He entertained millions, and his fans were passionate, ardent, and very much alive---as is Nelson's memory.

How did a star of Nelson's magnitude manage to live in the public eye for so many years and yet remain untainted?

One clue is the profound loyalty that all those who worked with him gave so willingly. Gale Sherwood performed with him for fourteen years in their nightclub act. His marriage to Ann was entering its twenty-eighth year when he died. His voice teacher and friend, Dr. Edouard Lippe, was with him for twenty-five years until his death. Ted Paxson, his accompanist and friend, was with Nelson for thirty-seven years. Art Rush spent twenty-two years as his manager, a lifetime as his friend. If there were complaints, they were seldom voiced. Nelson's demand for perfection was turned most often upon himself. His friends, neighbors, co-workers---every person who touched Nelson's life gave the same commentary.

For the most part, the good and decent live and die quietly. Little is written about them. "Good and decent" does not sell books! But, Nelson surely represents the exception as he possessed all the ideals that make America strong. He almost didn't have this tribute and it's partly his own fault! Nelson was a stickler for privacy. From the moment he stepped into the Hollywood arena, he refused to become an object of "idle gossip". Much of what's been written about him has never been substantiated. Plus, many of his friends have passed on without any serious efforts ever being made to set the record on Nelson straight.

That's where I come in. I missed the generation so devoted to him, but one night of late television viewing changed all that forever. Thanks to Turner Television Network, I was once again exposed to "that voice, those eyes, that hair, such a good and decent gentleman", who I knew instinctively to be all that and more.

Nelson's stepson Sidney Franklin, Jr. and his wife Janine, Gale Sherwood, Nelson's singing partner and Nelson's sister, Virginia Brown, have all been wonderful, giving and supportive to me.

I have interviewed many of Nelson's friends, those who knew him best, and let me tell you that he was just what my mother and those millions of fans described. Do you know how <u>rewarding</u> it is to start researching someone only to find out that they were exactly as people believed them to be.

Louella Parsons, the gossip columnist, claimed that Nelson Eddy was one of the few stars she never had to worry about. In the heyday of MGM, Louis B. Mayer would go to any extreme to protect the public image of his stars, and the studios were known to create "illusions of perfection" for the public. Nelson needed no protection. He was brilliant, vibrant, stalwart; not perfect---but closer than most.

For all of you who loved "the mountie" and what he stood for---here's to Nelson Eddy---a tribute!

Chapter One

New Year's Eve 1966 was a gala affair. All the world's problems were viewed with renewed hope as 1967 was about to be ushered in. The Grand Ballroom of the Waldorf-Astoria was packed with over 1200 revelers preparing to celebrate the coming event. The ballroom, ablaze with lights, glittering decorations and balloons suspended in huge fish nets, awaited the arrival of midnight. Guy Lombardo and his Royal Canadians were playing when it was announced that the television show would begin, and by some miraculous design, the dance floor cleared and a hush came over the crowd.

Nelson Eddy stepped on stage resplendent in a black tuxedo. Gold studs set with black onyx centers glistened from his white dress shirt. At 65, he was still extremely handsome though a little stouter, his fair hair tinged with gray. His magnetic presence silenced the crowd of merry-makers who suddenly sat still and attentive as his rich and compelling baritone filled the ballroom with a medley of old favorites. Gale Sherwood, his beautiful blonde singing partner of fourteen years, joined him on stage costumed in a shimmering gold sequined gown. As well as possessing a gloriously trained concert soprano voice, she is a brilliant comedienne and the perfect balance for Nelson's dignified persona. Tonight they sang many of the nostalgic duets of years gone by and the audience enthusiastically pleaded for more not realizing that their songs had been rehearsed and specifically timed to fit the program. After such well loved duets that recalled Nelson's movies such as *Sweethearts, One Alone* and *My Hero,* who could blame them?

That particular night Nelson was in wonderful spirits and he looked marvelous. Friends as well as fans were in attendance that New Year's Eve and he was genuinely glad to see them. Near the close of the television segment, Nelson and Gale mounted the bandstand to join Guy Lombardo and his singers in a rousing rendition of *Hello Dolly* and *Auld Lang Syne.* Nelson quietly stepped apart from the others on stage, slowly backing away from the microphone. He delighted the audience by unexpectedly directing them to join together in song and they happily complied.

Nelson and Gale shared a wonderful evening with their many fans. Nelson's happiness was so obviously in evidence that evening. This was the "pie ala mode" era of his life and he was enjoying every minute of it. He and Gale had built a highly successful nightclub act which mixed comic patter with new songs and old favorites. Their show was in such high demand that they were booked solidly for two years in advance.

Nelson and Gale were looking forward to their fourth Australian tour. They were extremely popular in Australia and although the tour was difficult and tiring, they were excited to return to their many fans there. Nelson was disappointed that his wife Ann had never been able to accompany him to Australia. He was anxious to share with her all the special places he had discovered and talked about with her. But it was not to be. When he performed in Australia during the 1964 tour, Ann had her bags packed, her ticket and visas all ready to go, when litigation over family property suddenly interrupted their plans. This time he realized that it was simply out of the question because of her recurring arthritis. The trip was strenuous enough for him and Gale, practiced as they were at handling the odd hours, large crowds and tiring travel schedules.

Alternate plans were made for Ann to join them between the Florida and Toronto club dates.

Right before the Australian trip, Nelson suffered through a draining bout of the flu and Gale had to have minor surgery. Then Ted Paxson became ill, and much to his dismay was unable to accompany them on tour for the first time in many years. With little time to spare, Nelson had to hire and train a new accompanist. The added stress of these misfortunes only added more zeal to Nelson's penchant for perfection. He worried all the way to Australia, and only when the plane landed did he finally give in to serendipity.

The Australian trip was excruciatingly demanding, but Nelson voiced no complaints. He met every scheduled appearance and performed eloquently. He was always pushing himself with that tremendous drive of his to overcome whatever complication barred his way, be it illness, back problems or lack of sleep. It was business as usual. He called Ann several times each day to keep her abreast of what was happening.

Any recognition or foreboding of events to come went unnoticed except for a comment made briefly one day while he and Gale stood before a mirror at the hotel. "My God Gale, look at my face and the puffs under my eyes. I'm really aging."

Pictures of Nelson on that three week Australian tour in January 1967 pointedly show a drastic change in his appearance. It's as if overnight he had aged. The buoyancy was gone, he looked wan and bedraggled. But his wholesome friendliness and beautiful voice stayed ever intact. Gale noticed a slight difference, especially the puffiness under his eyes, but nothing was mentioned between them. There were schedules to be kept, planes to catch, interviews to give and performances, performances, performances.

To the audiences, fans and critics, this fourth trip to Australia was an all time high. Their appearance at "Chequers" in Sydney broke the house record for capacity crowds. Ed Sullivan wrote in his New York column, "Nelson Eddy a roaring hit in Australia." The Daily Mirror wrote, "Nelson Eddy and Gale Sherwood give a magnificent performance. It is enough to say that these two wonderful artists have never been better."

During one interview, on January 17, 1967, Nelson drew attention to his own epitaph by asking a reporter, "At the end of my life, when you come to write my occupation, I hope you will describe me as a *concert* performer and not a film star. I was a concert performer long before I was a film star and a stage performer for a long time afterwards." These were to become prophetic words.

Nelson and Gale returned to the States exhilarated, but totally exhausted. Their schedule didn't allow them much time for a needed rest. They were able to spend one short week at home in Los Angeles before leaving for Florida on March 4th. They were to perform at the Sans Souci Hotel in Miami Beach, Florida on March fifth and then continue on to Canada for their other scheduled club dates. Two performances were scheduled at the Sans Souci. In the early afternoon Nelson took his usual "daily constitutional", dressed for the show, and called Ann one last time before the performance.

Ann was relieved he was back in the States. She always worried about the long trips. The short ones were much easier to handle. She was used to being alone for short periods and secure in their lifestyle after many years of marriage. The months ahead would be busily filled with their grandchildren's birthdays and many plans to share together. Nelson received two calls from Ann on Saturday evening, March 4th. He wrote her a short note that evening. They loved to send articles to each other. Telephone calls and letters always flowed between them while Nelson was on the road.

Before an enthusiastic crowd of 400, Nelson and Gale started their act. Gale remembers that night very vividly. It was to be the last time they would perform together. By 8:00 the next morning Nelson was gone and an era was ended.

Jeanette MacDonald, Nelson's movie partner and the other half of "America's Singing Sweethearts", had passed away two years before after suffering from a heart condition. She died at the age of fifty-seven on January 14th, 1965, while awaiting open-heart surgery in a Houston hospital.

Now with both of their passing, our illusions of the fabled screen lovers had come to an end. The world had changed remarkably, the turbulent 60's fostered an awakening of our social consciousness and divided us over the Vietnam war. But the Nelson Eddy remembered is the Nelson of a more gracious time when those "Singing Sweethearts" guided us softly through the long bleak years of the depression. A little bit of America died with them. There was a collective lump in the throats of those 40 and older. Schmaltz? Yes, but not to a generation who knew misery and found beauty.

In 1935, film director, Robert Z. Leonard chose his all-time best screen teams. Myrna Loy and William Powell as "the marrieds", Robert Taylor and Greta Garbo as "the lovers" and Nelson Eddy and Jeanette MacDonald as "prince and princess charming". No other team ever topped the Eddy-MacDonald combination in their appeal or their beautifully blended voices.

These are the memories of a whole generation. Could it all have happened so long ago; it seems like only yesterday. We never really forget; in fact, with each passing year, the past seems to grow brighter for those of us who need to see it as though it were only yesterday.

For when we are young, we want to grow old, and as time passes, we delight in remembering when we were young. The memories are often bittersweet, for we had passion then and we had heroes. Thelma Cohen remembers the first time she actually met Nelson Eddy. She later became president of Nelson's fan club for many years until his death.

> It was April 1944, at Carnegie Hall, New York City. He'd sung in concert and performed to a capacity audience, and at the conclusion of his recital, many of us went backstage. He was seated at a small writing table giving the requested autographs, shaking hands with those speaking to him. I shall always remember "the shock" of actually coming face to face with him; he was pale and obviously weary, but the patience and warmth of his smile and those deep, dark blue eyes that looked right into mine were captivating. I couldn't possibly recall what I said or what he said, it was like a dream come true and, oh, so brief. But the encounter has stayed with me these 45 years, and I can still see him as clearly as if it were yesterday.

Barbara Butler, a fan, expressed her feelings in the Chicago Tribune not long after Nelson's death:

> I saw each of their movies 20 or 30 times until I knew all the lines by heart. My girl friend Ellen and I would take our lunches and would be waiting at the box office the minute it opened in the morning. We would emerge at night nearly blinded, but superbly

happy, warbling the tuneful melodies all the way home. Later we learned the words to all their songs and sang duets on every possible occasion. Our favorite practicing place was our church rest room where the acoustics enriched and enlarged our voices until we could imagine that we approached the splendor of the MacDonald-Eddy voices.

The high point of those years came just before graduation and could have caused the one blemish on my quite impeccable record if the school had found out. Nelson Eddy came to town for a concert, and Ellen and I recklessly feigned illness to go to his hotel. We had no thought of bothering him, only to be near him. Although the hotel was not giving out information, we rode up and down the elevator until by sheer good luck we overheard an elevator boy tell a reporter which room was his. Shaking with excitement, we crept up to his door (HIS DOOR) and listened. Then, unbelievably, we heard that rich, beautiful baritone voice that we knew as well as each other's! Suddenly, my knees buckled, and Ellen had to support me to keep me from sagging to the floor.

From that experience, we ascended even higher to the ecstasy of the concert that night. We were awed by his dignity and thrilled by his handsome appearance as he strode onto the stage, impressively dressed in tails. The critics said that he sang magnificently, but he did more than that for us. We saw our ideal in the flesh and the moment was sublime.

And I may weep some more, partly for them and partly for myself and all those who cannot bear to relinquish their youth and its dreams. But I will always remember.

"A Golden Gift
A life well spent
If everyone could boast the same
Their rest would be content."
Author Unknown

CHAPTER TWO

Nelson Eddy described his stardom as the success that "merely happened" and became the envy of thousands of aspiring singers in this country as well as the unwilling recipient of adulation by millions of women during the Golden Era of Entertainment. The story of Nelson, classical singer, movie star, radio personality, night club entertainer, gentlemen and nice person, is the saga of a true American abundant with all the fine traditions of his English ancestry.

New England at the turn of the century was experiencing tremendous industrial development. But, in keeping with the Victorian era just past, Puritan ethics were still intact. Morality and decency were encouraged, while a conscious rectitude was considered admirable. Strict religious training was a priority in most homes.

It was into this cozy and secure environment of soft-toned structure that Nelson descended on June 29, 1901 in the New England town of Providence, Rhode Island. Providence was a bustling and friendly town built around three large hills. By the year 1900, Providence was firmly entrenched in the Industrial Revolution, busily growing in prosperity.

Nelson's parents had already established themselves in Providence before Nelson's birth. William Darius Eddy was a machinist and part-time musician, and Providence offered a plentiful bounty of jobs for him. Any free time found Bill assisting in the many musical productions staged in and around Providence. Nelson's mother, Caroline Isabel Kendrick was the well-bred and beautiful daughter of Carolyn Ackerman Kendrick a singer of oratorios. Of strong Dutch descent, Isabel was born and raised in Atlanta, Georgia and is joined by ancestral lineage to our eighth president, Martin Van Buren.

They met while Bill was stationed in Georgia during the Spanish-American War. It was their shared love of music that had brought them together but then Bill suffered a harrowing battle with typhoid fever in late 1898 and almost died. The family still has a copy of his "obituary" which the local paper published on the belief he wouldn't live through the night.

Shored up by the love of his beautiful Isabel and a tough constitution, Bill fought the disease and won. While recuperating at the Army hospital in Georgia, their brief war-time romance intensified. Isabel was nineteen and Bill twenty-four when they married on December 23, 1899. They moved into a rented home at 26 Harford Avenue in the Johnson section of Providence just a few feet west of Olneyville Square.

Even Nelson's ancestors were of staunch and proper bearing. Samuel Eddye had arrived in colonial Massachusetts sometime in the sixteenth century, and although he missed the Mayflower by almost ten years, he married and settled down in what is now Middleboro, Massachusetts where he continued to propagate the ancestral roots. Several of his grandchildren later moved to Providence where today, Eddy Street is named after one of his grandsons. After two generations, the English "e" in Eddye was dropped.

In 1900, only 8000 people owned cars and America boasted 400 college graduates. It was a time of music in the parlor, country outings, tennis on the lawn and teas by the riverbank. Most families traveled by horse and buggy or street cars to the church socials and sporting events. A woman's place was definitely in the home; long skirts and big hats were the style of the day and manners were strongly adhered to by all.

Nelson celebrated his birth with a loud and lusty scream. Isabel Eddy recalled the doctor making only one comment at the time. "Good lungs," he proclaimed with a smile of satisfaction. There was nothing outstanding or momentous in Nelson's childhood. He was a sturdy, stocky little boy who possessed an unusual habit of bursting into song much of the time. In keeping with the Victorian era just past, strict rules and moralizing were fostered in the home. One can picture Nelson at the dinner table, well scrubbed, mannerly and obedient to authority.

Those first years were carefree---kites, pocket knives, roller skates and "kick the can" were favorite past times along with boating and fishing on Narragansett Bay and playing baseball in Roger Williams Park. Although a serious child, he developed quite a flair for light humor at an early age. There was always music around him, and on quiet evenings, he and his mother played the piano and sang hymns. He also had fond memories of spending weekends with his paternal grandparents in Pawtucket. He credits them with his reverence of old things, which he valued all his life...the gentleness, kindness and reverence to God which encircled the basic simplicity of life they valued. It is evident that throughout Nelson's life, each time he became immersed in the materialistic state of "stardom" and the accompanying hero-worship, he would restrict his egoism and all material excess and return to a simpler, more comfortable state of being.

Those early years, until it was time for Nelson to go school, were for the most part peaceful and uneventful. His tapestry of shadowed memories seemed to revolve around an old New England house, a dark-haired father who was strong but most kindly, and a lovely petite auburn-haired mother who was to him "the comfort of life".

In an interview given to Howard Sharp in August of 1936, Nelson related a conscious memory that seems to remain his only outstanding remembrance of those early childhood days:

> I had been left alone for a little while and the need for search and exploration possessed me suddenly, so what is it you do at that age, toddle? I toddled right out of the room, down the hall and stairs and through an open door. There was a garden around the place. I puttered there for awhile and then I found a gate. It seems to me that I went miles down the road, but probably I was about 50 yards from the house when I realized the place that had sheltered me all my life was lost somewhere and that I didn't even know how to get back to it. Something, an entirely horrible emotion, enclosed me. I sat down and howled, as I was terrified. Then I heard a voice, arms caught me up, and my mother made little astonished but reassuring noises to me. It was like being saved from drowning when you have given up hope!

Perhaps there is a deeper meaning in that story, as Nelson and his mother maintained an exceptionally close relationship which offered them a friendship of equality that was to last all the years of her life.

From the early beginning of Nelson's childhood, it was established that Isabel Eddy possessed the ability to instill in Nelson the qualities of love and self esteem, and through that simple love, he responded by believing that she was forever in support of him. She possessed a depth of faith and understanding which gave him strength to persevere over impossible obstacles. And that understanding and faith became a part of Nelson's own philosophy. Bill brought his own special gifts into Nelson's life. He deeply loved Nelson and also admired his talent, but it was Bill's dry wit mixed with his military demeanor that influenced Nelson's character. Nelson began to know himself and believe in himself on the gentle promise that if parents as loving, intelligent and caring as his could find merit in his talents ---then surely---it must be true.

Five years into the marriage, it was apparent to both Isabel and William that they were drifting apart. Their wartime romance, fueled by the uncertainties of life and death, and their shared love of music were not enough to build a marriage upon. Isabel intuitively knew that she was dealing with not one, but two dilemmas; a fragile marriage and a son who loved to sing. How could she solve both, since the two problems were not at all compatible?

Still, Nelson's environment continued to be nourished by music and this effort was shared by both of his parents. In 1900, one million families owned a piano. The piano so dominated every parlor that Ladies Home Journal wrote special articles on "How to Decorate the Instrument". It was natural to teach and educate your child in music especially if talent was inherited. Not only was Nelson's grandmother a distinguished oratorio singer, but his paternal grandfather and namesake, Isaac Nelson Eddy was a bass drummer with Reeves American Band for fifty-five years. Isaac spent long hours teaching Nelson the drum rhythms, and Nelson later played trap drums in the school orchestra. Isabel herself was a soloist in her church, The Church of the Transfiguration, in Providence.

Nelson's father was a noted choir singer and stage performer as well as a stagehand at the Providence Opera House. He could play any musical instrument he tried, but his love was the pipe organ. He also became a drum major of the 1st Regimental Coast Artillery Band of the Rhode

Island National Guard. In fact, when Nelson was young, he went to camp with his dad as the "camp mascot". Nelson and Bill recalled many happy memories from those summers together. There was the time Nelson refused to learn how to swim and Bill Eddy took him out in a rowboat and threw him in the water. Nelson was so mad, he swam all the way back to shore. When he was eight-years old he sang his first real solo, *The Lost Chord,* while at Fort Greble with his father.

But underneath the calm lay the unresolved conflicts in the marriage and the added stress of frequent moves. As a machinist for the Naval Torpedo Station in Newport, Bill became more involved in the manufacturing of torpedo devices for the navy while Isabel grew even more and more restless.

Nelson was a very intelligent child, but unfortunately, he never had the opportunity to really excel because he changed schools so often. In the classrooms, even whispering merited a whipping. The McGuffey's Reader that Nelson studied praised the rewards of virtuous behavior and warned that lazy children would come to no good and Nelson took each word seriously.

He attended four different schools in eight years---New Bedford's Dartmouth Street Primary School, Rhode Island Normal School, Providence Edgewood Grammar School, and Grove Street Grammar School in Pawtucket. The one constant ingredient in his life was music and both parents continued to steadfastly encourage his participation. During their joint singing and playing, Isabel began to teach Nelson the nuances of music. Another talent began to define itself during Nelson's childhood; his ability to draw. In the right educational and financial atmosphere, Nelson would have been described as a child prodigy.

In Nelson's mind, the early part of his childhood was divided into three classifications. In an interview with Howard Sharp, Nelson listed, "The summer interludes on the beautiful New England farm of his great grandmother in Acushnet, Massachusetts; the fascinating home of his paternal grandparents; the grammar schools of which there were so many" and alongside these remembrances, there was the insistent need for music and art.

When Nelson was small and went to visit the farm of Great-grandma and Great-grandpa Gardiner, Grandma Eddy's parents, they would make it a special occasion for him.

Time stopped for Nelson during those lovely visits, and all through his life, if he would catch a faint smell of ginger or hear a certain little song, he would remember himself coming across the meadow and through the orchards for dinner. He remembered the dimly lit attic loft crowded with discarded objects and old trunks. He could still visualize large bowls of chrysanthemums and smell the scent of spices in the air. There was an old family rocking horse, and of course, the huge bible placed lovingly atop the old pedal organ. It was a time of hymns, church, home-baked foods and soft feather beds. There was a simple grace at every meal. As Nelson noted often, "They were nice things to remember...these were the simplest of joys".

These visits also offered Nelson a reprieve from the harsher realities in his life which were caused by the family's inner conflicts. Nelson had to go through the pain often inflicted on the "new boy" at any school. There was always the process of having to prove oneself or letting people know who you are or having to stand aside in loneliness while the other kids decide whether they like you or not.

These experiences also helped to mold Nelson's personality; he was able to walk a solitary path whenever necessary and pull within himself for private introspection. He was hesitant to form deeper friendships because he knew he could not keep them. However, his heart did surrender to the sweet and beguiling ways of one very special young lady. Her name was Alma Wilcox and she became his one and only childhood sweetheart. By 1910, the comic strip and baseball cards were invented. The Boy Scouts were just starting to form nationwide, but Nelson was never able to enjoy the warm bonds cultivated by such an experience.

He turned more and more to music---music which was the motivating force of his existence. From his earliest memory, it had seeped into his consciousness, and now it began to possess him. Music was a constant---it was everywhere in his life. Grandma Eddy even gave him piano lessons, but Nelson was usually too busy to practice. Yet he always found time to sing. In the afternoons and early evenings he and Isabel would sit and sing quiet duets of simple hymns of the Christian faith. To Isabel and Bill, it was obvious that Nelson was quite gifted. He had a beautiful voice----a soprano voice at that!

In 1911, when Nelson was ten, he was given an audition to sing in the boy's choir at St. Steven's Episcopal Church. He made it on the first try. He loved singing in the choir, but during the sermons he used to read the funny papers. Isabel, firmly committed to furthering Nelson's talent, searched for a good choir director for him. At Grace Church, an organist by the name of Arthur Lacey-Baker took an avid interest in Nelson. Arthur Lacey-Baker developed Nelson's voice for two years and helped him formulate his tonal quality well enough to become the church's youngest soprano soloist. Then in 1913, he began singing at All Saints Church. Nelson always felt that, by going from church to church, he had been exposed to so many versions of religion in his early years, that in later life he evolved his own deep belief in God---a philosophy which permeated every aspect of his life.

Yet Nelson for his part was more settled in school than at any other time. Settled in Pawtucket for several years, Nelson loved the hills that sloped gently towards the rivers. An industrial city, it depended on the fortunes or misfortunes of the textile industry. Grandpa Eddy was President of the Pawtucket Ice Company and they lived at 58 Myrtle Street. Nelson was over at Grandma and Grandpa Eddys so often that Grandpa recorded his growth on their kitchen door frame. It was still etched on the door when the family finally sold the house in 1973.

His hair by now was bright red, and the children taunted him with nicknames such as "brick-top" and "carrot-head". Nelson chose to deal with the name calling by simply pulling back and walking his solitary path. This characteristic became known in later years as his system of "stoic resolve". Every once in awhile, he would get into a scuffle or a fight. Being sturdy and robust, he managed quite well. There were a few times he lost the fight, but at least he went into battle.

One Sunday, when he was singing his solo, Nelson recalled, "My vibrant high 'C' slipped miserably into an 'A' flat and then completely cracked, becoming a thin squeak". It was apparent to his parents, the choir director, and flustered congregation that Nelson's voice had reached puberty. It was decided that Nelson should definitely not sing for a couple of years. Nelson recognized the importance of this decision and agreed. He was at an age where other priorities occupied his time; Nelson had his good friends and a few favorite teachers. He preferred to read, draw and make gadgets. He was so good in woodworking that the manual arts teacher made him his first assistant. Nelson was looking forward to attending the technical high school and studying manual arts. However, it was the fair-haired girls that unnerved him. He had spent little time around girls and was quite self-conscious with them.

At the same time, Isabel and Bill began to resolve the problems of their floundering marriage. They both had grave concerns for their son as well as for each other. Being sensible and religious people, they agreed that a better life would exist for all concerned if they were to lead it separately.

So, soon after his graduation from Grove Street Grammar School, his parents sat him down to discuss their ultimate decision. All his other concerns, including his shyness around the opposite sex, became minimal as the reality of their decision began to take its affect on him.

At fourteen, Nelson was faced with the prospect of leaving school forever, thereby giving up any chance for a formal education. He would leave his friends and comforts behind to start a new life in Philadelphia. More importantly, he would take on the responsibility of a full time job. The family had little money. In order to make ends meet, their choices were few....to buy bare necessities, sacrifices had to be made. Nelson sadly and unhappily accepted his fate.

Bill Eddy was most affected by the trauma of the breakup. He lost the opportunity to influence his son's life and share with him the everyday happenings that bond a father and son together.

However, it is a credit to both parents and their relationship with each other that Nelson bore no serious scars on his mind or soul. Bill and "Belle", as he called her, remained friends throughout their lives. Their shared love for Nelson remained the bond between them.

Chapter Three

Isabel and Nelson moved to Philadelphia late in the summer of 1915; however, the divorce wasn't finalized until April 24, 1918. Isabel took a job with the University of Pennsylvania, and Nelson went to work for Clark Kendrick, Isabel's brother, who managed the Mott Iron Works. Nelson never returned to school. He continued to keep in touch with Alma, either by letter or through his father. Bill Eddy was very fond of her and held high hopes that they would marry some day.

Desperately wanting to continue his education, Nelson voraciously worked his way through a multitude of correspondence courses. Nelson believed that the object of education was to train the whole moral and intelligent being ---not just the intellect. By age sixteen, he had completed courses on science, art, biology, psychology and several languages. He read "The Wealth of Nations" by Adam Smith and "Plutarch". No small feat on their own merit, he studied these courses while working at the iron works. His sketches and drawings at that time were considered very advanced for his age. The neatly tied diplomas offer ample proof that, at a young age, he possessed the tenacity and hard driven determination which would later lead him to an even greater destiny. He would remain an avid reader throughout his life and digested information on every topic imaginable.

By now he and Isabel had settled into a small apartment. Nelson spent every spare minute along with every spare dime to study, sketch or attend as many concerts and operettas as were available to him. His artwork was proudly displayed on the empty walls of their new home...except for his nudes which the genteel Isabel insisted he keep hidden in his art portfolio. To this day many of Nelson's avant-garde nudes are coveted by family and friends.

His first job at the Mott Iron Works plant was as a telephone operator. In current terminology, he was a customer service representative. By now his voice had settled into a bass-baritone. He immediately began to sing again. Singing was free. It didn't cost any money, and it brought him great joy. Customers were quite disconcerted by Nelson's bursts of melody when all they wanted was a keg of nails or a case of bolts. So Clark Kendrick decided it would be in everyone's best interest if he transferred Nelson to the shipping department where his voice would be better contained. Nelson really kicked up his heels at this, mainly because he hated the work. There must be a more enjoyable way to pay the bills.

He would have made a great drummer; he loved the feel and the control of the rhythmic sticks. He had become quite a skilled drummer. Ever since Grandpa Eddy had taught him to play the trap drums as a child, he would find a piano player wherever he could and match his rhythms to the cords. He was thrilled when offered an opportunity to play the drums in Jenkinstown, Pennsylvania, but on the very night he was to audition, the plant foreman made him work overtime. As a result, the world lost a very good drummer, and the mill lost a good employee. Nelson had finally had it....he up and quit!

Dejected and depressed, he withdrew into himself. Financially, the family depended upon his salary. Where was he to find a job that would bring him satisfaction as well. His next try was banking, but the timing was all wrong; no one was hiring. After weeks of searching for work, he finally landed a job with "The Philadelphia Press" as a night clerk for eight dollars a week. Isabel continued to believe in her son's musical talent and prayed for the professional training he so desperately needed. Nelson would later comment "My strong dash of Dutch ancestry was just enough to take the color out of my eyebrows and perhaps it accounts for a certain stubborn stick-to-it quality that has always ruled my life." It's that quality that kept Nelson singing and believing.

Nelson's habit of bursting into song continued everywhere he went. His family's musical heritage had surely provided him the talent, but he had no means of professional entre. Nelson kept working and studying while continuing to hold onto his dream of obtaining a professional voice teacher. He made home recordings to aid in learning new songs. One home recording he composed himself was called *The Rainbow Trail*.

A reporter friend of Nelson's suggested he could make extra money by writing obituaries and offered to teach him. After a few lessons, Nelson developed quite a flair. The commissions he earned helped ease the financial burdens a bit. He was now sixteen years old but looked to be at least nineteen.

Ever undaunted, Nelson decided it was time to try something new. One particular morning, he awoke with added zest for life and renewed hope in his heart. He convinced the city editor of the "Evening Public Ledger" in Philadelphia to give him a staff position---his first newspaper job! Unfortunately, several weeks later, the newspaper underwent a staff reduction which put Nelson right back on the street. But Nelson was bitten by the journalism bug. He found the newspaper office appealing.

He talked with the editor of the "Evening Bulletin" and persuaded the editor into believing he was a "crack reporter". A former co-worker was to remark later that

Nelson was a hell of a good reporter and a regular guy---his friends dubbed him "the singing reporter". At sixteen, he was reporting the news on sports, politics, deaths, and any police news he could get his hands on. He found the job interesting and exciting. He even worked as a cashier and night clerk for the paper on his off hours. He really had something to sing about. His habit of bursting into song continued---why, he even sang at the copy desk and lived to tell about it, much to the dismay and awe of all those around him.

No closer to his goal than before, he continued to sing with Isabel, and her optimism and belief in him never faltered. The social mores of the 1920's demanded that young people attend formal parties and dances. Nelson frequently attended the social dances. He was tall with reddish hair and appeared to the young ladies as a quiet, introverted young man. He and Alma still kept in touch, but the relationship was destined to end. He had no time for romance in his life.

One night while listening to Ruffo sing an aria, he was so inspired that he began to sing along with the trained voice of Ruffo's. Still reeling from this new found excitement, he rushed out the next day, bought all the records he could find of the great baritones of the day and he began to sing with them. From these records, he imitated the voices of Ruffo, Scotti, Amato, Campanari, and Werrenrath and so began his next attempt in self education. This inspiration landed Nelson right into total financial straits. Consciously or subconsciously, Nelson was allowing music to take full command of his life. He was tormented by his desire and the everyday struggles to survive which pulled him away from his dreams. He was told by others to "give it up". He abused his voice unknowingly by placing it at the wrong level. There were many times when he simply gave up believing in the silent possibility of the impossible.

Isabel was singing at the Church of the Savior in Philadelphia at this time and it was there she and Nelson met Gertrude Cheshire Evans, a socialite and internationally known bridge player. A close friendship developed between Gertrude and Isabel. She was to play an important role in Nelson's struggle to succeed.

In November 1920, he quit the newspaper for a job as a copy writer with the N. W. Ayer Advertising Agency. This job offered him a little bit higher pay but, more importantly, allowed him more free time to sing. It wasn't long before the advertising agency took a good look at their new employee and decided that he was far more interested in music than he was in copyrighting or advertising. When he wasn't racking his brains for adjectives to describe the products, he would sing. Years later he was to run into his old boss who lovingly wisecracked, "Nelson, that singing drove me crazy!"

It was at this critical point in Nelson's life that he met David Bispham, one of the great baritones of his age. Gertrude Evans and David Bispham were friends and she set up the meeting for Nelson. Nelson viewed this meeting as a true and bonafide miracle. Determined to seize the opportunity, he immediately asked Bispham for an audition. Bispham generously agreed, and upon hearing Nelson sing an Italian aria he had memorized, Bispham responded, "Almost, but not quite." He told Nelson, "You must study, study, study". Nelson, ever grateful, heard the message loud and clear. The sixty-year old former opera singer convinced Nelson to study with him, but the fortuitous relationship was short lived because Bispham died in October, 1921.

Just when the world appeared darkest and all appeared lost, another miracle occurred. It was 1922 and

Mrs. George Dallas Dixon's Society was producing a musical called "The Marriage Tax" at the Philadelphia Academy of Music. Nelson auditioned and won the role of the King of Greece....he was a smashing success! Accidentally, his name was somehow omitted from the program. This "accident" proved most fortunate because, when all the reporters and critics were writing up their reviews of "The Marriage Tax", they wanted to know the identity of the mystery baritone with the marvelous voice. Thus, Nelson received his first real publicity!

Actually, this semi-professional musical society sparked him into taking serious singing lessons and also gave him a deeper belief in his own talents. It was at this time that other events were also unfolding in Nelson's personal life. Several years after his divorce, Bill Eddy had met Marguerite Elliott at St. George Episcopal in Newport where they both sang in the church choir. She was a bacteriologist for the city of Newport. Nelson had met Marguerite on several occasions and was delighted when they announced their wedding date. Unfortunately, it was impossible for him to attend the ceremony at Vassar College on June 13, 1923 because of a singing engagement. He felt an immense duty towards his family and not being at his father's wedding ceremony caused much pain and disappointment to both father and son. Everyone recognized that a career demanded such sacrifices, but for Bill Eddy, any time with Nelson was a precious commodity ---he had lost so much of Nelson because of the divorce. Realizing the tenuous situation, Nelson visited his father and Marguerite immediately after his concert.

Not long after Nelson returned to Philadelphia, he was introduced to Alexander Smallens, the director of the Philadelphia Civic Opera Company. Alexander was attracted to Nelson because of his outstanding performance in "The Marriage Tax". Smallens was to become Nelson's first patron. He began to give Nelson serious coaching and it was under his direction that Nelson toiled through twenty-three operatic roles. Another fortuitous event occurred when Gertrude Evans opened her home to Isabel and Nelson. At her insistence they lived with the Evans family while Nelson studied with Smallens.

All the heartache and struggle paid off for Nelson in 1924 when he won his first operatic role as Amonasro in "Aida" at the Philadelphia Civic Opera. The "Philadelphia Record" wrote glowingly: "Nelson Eddy, as Amonasro, had an electrifying effect on the audience. A young singer, with that indefinable gift so seldom seen of arresting the audience's interest and holding it continuously, Mr. Eddy was a star from the moment he appeared on the stage. His enunciation alone was a distinguishing mark, every syllable being easily understood, while his acting was spontaneous and natural."

Nelson also won the lead in Gilbert and Sullivan's "Iolanthe" at the Savoy Opera Company. The Savoy often gave opportunities to aspiring professionals and Nelson, once again, was a tremendous success. Of his performance in Iolanthe, the "Philadelphia Evening Bulletin" wrote: "Of the male members of the cast, a notable success may be credited to Nelson Eddy, who, as Strephon, the hapless shepherd---half fairy, half mortal---has none of the crudeness or uncertainly of the amateur, either as actor or singer. Easy, graceful, and showing an excellent understanding of all he has to do, Mr. Eddy fills his part without effort, and not in a long time has there been revealed a baritone voice of greater beauty, of fresh, sympathetic quality, excellent volume and range, and evidently of great possibilities." Alexander Smallens, pleased with his protege, also gave

Nelson additional parts in a little theatre group called "Plays and Players".

Things were happening so fast, one can't help but wonder if, about this time, Philadelphia had discovered that Nelson was listed in the social register. After all, his family was one of the founders of the Colonies. Philadelphia was suddenly showering Nelson with opportunities. Nelson gave his all at every performance. He became a success in his own right, and to him, he had found heaven on earth!

At twenty-three, he was described as a serious student of music, and his commitment would bring magnificent results in later years. He developed a naturalness about himself and began to feel comfortable in front of large groups of people. He was beginning to shave off the rough edges of a most complex personality. As he matured, he put into action all the qualities and characteristics which he had developed earlier in life. There were multiple machineries that made Nelson tick and they began to synchronize their parts to form a perfect timing. One got the feeling that he was almost too perfect, "such a well-balanced person...too big, too genuine, too easy to understand after a quick survey". Nothing was farther from the truth. Nelson was very complex, but he was in the process of discovering a unique ability which allowed just the right part of his personality to be matched to just the right occasion. The public was beginning to take notice.

Another member of the opera company was Dr. Edouard Lippe, a veteran opera singer. They met professionally while Nelson was singing in "Tannhauser". Nelson relates the story that he had just completed his part in "Tannhauser" and actually had his back turned to Lippe when he heard a voice behind him say, "You have a nice voice Mr. Eddy, but you don't know how to use it." Nelson, upset by this presumption and feeling quite self-conscious, turned to face the little man and simply gave him a look of annoyance. However, that very night while performing, he sang off key. He already had grave doubts about his talent and Dr. Lippe's comments had unnerved him. The whole episode disturbed him so greatly that he called Lippe the very next day to ask if they might meet.

Lippe might have been a great artist himself for he certainly had the voice, but he had injured his spine in a boyhood bicycle accident which severely affected his physique, so he had turned to teaching. As timing and fate would have it, Lippe the great teacher and Nelson the great singer, came together to form a relationship that would last all their lives.

Nelson continued to work days, study his correspondence courses or draw at night and sing at any opportunity he could find. Isabel continued to encourage and support his determination. A pleasant surprise occurred when, on February 21, 1926, Nelson was greeted with the news that he had a half-sister named Martha Virginia. Possessing a deep love of family, Nelson was ecstatic. Despite the difference in age and lifestyles, Nelson became a distant, yet loving and generous older brother for the rest of his life. Although "Ginny" was his half sister, he warmly referred to her as his "kid sister". After Ginny's birth, the Eddys moved to Jamestown, Rhode Island where they lived until 1937.

On the advice of Dr. Lippe, Nelson decided to seek instruction from one of the famous voice teachers in Philadelphia at that time, a man by the name of William Vilonat. Although Lippe was a strong influence in Nelson's life, Nelson continued to drive himself endlessly. It was Lippe who warned Nelson that if he continued to work himself so hard, he would not only lose his voice, but very possibly his life.

Edouard Lippe was a strong personality in his own right and it should be said that over the years, Edouard and Nelson had many temperamental feuds. They always settled their battles and in doing so strengthened their deep friendship. Besides---Lippe usually won anyway!

When Vilanot announced he was leaving for Dresden to work with serious voice students, it was Lippe who convinced Nelson to borrow on his future. Nelson turned to Roland Taylor, a Philadelphia banker and family friend, for a loan of $8,000.00 to finance his musical education. In 1927, Nelson accompanied Vilonat to Europe while Isabel remained in the Evans' home.

They reached Dresden in early summer and Nelson found the huge city to be crowded with buildings and only a few trees sparsely shading the streets. It might have been somewhat difficult for him to leave his friends and his home for all of this, but he knew instinctively that he had come for only one reason---to work. His mind and soul engulfed in one goal---to sing. He boarded with a kind German family in an old rambling house. Although he was tired and depleted after long hours of study, he would sing favorite Viennese and German songs for his new family and their friends. Many late evenings were spent gathered around the parlor piano. He had audiences again and he loved them.

It didn't matter to Nelson whether Dresden was made of rain or sunshine, because he never saw any of it. The months that followed were a constant dedication and determination to only one effort---to study voice. He learned the scores of operettas in four languages; he experimented with arrangements; he discovered lyric control and he learned how to breath properly. Vilanot was a very patient although sometimes frenzied teacher; there was no rest for Nelson. Vilanot sternly lectured, "There is no time, and you haven't much money. You have to use every second. There are no hours to spare for anything else."

Every once in awhile, Nelson would manage to get a glimpse of life in the beer gardens and the lighthearted fun people his age were having. They were enjoying their youth while it lasted, but not Nelson!

He grew a little thinner, sang a little better and lost himself in his music. One night near the end of Nelson's training with Vilanot, the chubby little Scandinavian hesitantly approached Nelson, "Please before you leave for America, I would like you to do me a favor," he smiled. "Three girl pupils of mine are having auditions at the Dresden Opera, and it would please me if you would be one of my boys, just to prove to those generals that I can teach men in the art of singing as well as women." Of course, Nelson, always willing to please, agreed. He thought it was a clever gag! So that night, in slight repayment for all of Vilanot's friendship, Nelson appeared on stage at the Royal Dresden Opera and resolutely sang his heart out.

After the audition, Nelson forgot singing---he badly needed a rest. His mother and uncle had come to Germany to meet him and they planned to travel France and England together before sailing home to the states. After two weeks of vacation it was time to say goodbye to Vilanot before leaving for home. When Nelson called on Vilanot, he was shocked to be greeted with a huge hug as Vilanot exclaimed, "You are chosen to be the next great opera star of Europe! They gave you the role in the Dresden Opera Company."

Nelson in total astonishment said, "What role, what are you talking about?" "At the Dresden Opera," Vilanot howled, "you are to be the leading baritone there. It is the beginning of your career, all because of that fake audition I asked you to do."

Nelson did what might appear to many as a totally insane thing; he simply refused the job! Vilanot pleaded and stormed, but to no avail. Nelson was home sick and wanted to return to the states. Sadly, Vilanot never forgave him. Vilanot, like Bispham, died before Nelson reached his professional heights of stardom.

Nelson returned to his own teacher, Dr. Lippe, and continued to appear with the Philadelphia Opera. He performed roles in "Feuersnot", Strauss's "Ariadne auf Naxos" and "Adriadne". Nelson was anxious to work; he even hired a manager by the name of Calvin Franklin. His first priority was to repay his kind and trusting benefactor, Roland Taylor, who had lent him the money to study in Europe. He also owed much to Gertrude Evans and her husband who had opened their home to them and eased the financial burden on Nelson and Isabel.

Nelson's decision to return home to America was very fortuitous. He said at the time, "I just wanted to see America again. I wanted to put myself in the hands of the American public, sink or swim." It was a time in America when concert singers were very majestic, very formal. They sang the usual standardized classical routine with an air of condescension to impress the audience. It was in this milieu that Nelson began to tour the country and to sing anywhere and everywhere he could. However, Nelson was different; he emanated genuineness and warmth. The very qualities which were naturally innate in his personality became even more magnified by his understated ego.

He and Isabel settled into a spacious apartment on 13th and Chestnut Streets in Philadelphia, but he wasn't able to enjoy it very much; he was always concertizing. Local concert managers began to ask for the handsome young baritone with the ringing voice. Nelson became well known through his audiences because of the intimacy he weaved with them. It was the concert stage that would bring Nelson to the attention of Hollywood not so many years later.

Chapter Four

Nelson hit the musical world by storm. In 1928, he sang for manager Arthur Judson of Columbia Concerts. Judson was quick to recognize Nelson's talent and unique abilities; he signed him with Columbia Concerts and Nelson made his first concert appearance in Norristown, Pennsylvania. Nelson developed and perfected twenty-eight operas and eleven oratorios. His repertoire also included countless numbers of art songs, popular classics and even the operetta favorites. He loved concertizing. He would perform, race to catch a train, study, practice and be ready to perform again the next night. How he maintained this level of energy is hard to determine---but he never faltered. He was young and beautiful; women began to follow him everywhere.

Money was not a priority---he hoped for $50 per concert and was happy to get $25. Something else was happening to Nelson's soul during these concerts. Primarily, Nelson was a toiler. He was used to working long hours, but he consciously discovered that unless he was working, he tended to fall into distracted moods. Ah....but when he sang, he became a warm and peaceful soul filled with happiness. From the first time any sound came from his lungs, it gave him a fullness of life that nothing else was ever capable of giving to him.

Nelson constantly worked on all aspects of his singing. He always looked at the whole picture and reached for total perfection. One of Nelson's principal assets, both in opera and in concert, was his diction. He enunciated his words so clearly that they were understood without sacrifice of tonal quality.

In 1929, Nelson met a twenty-six year old pianist by the name of Theodore Paxson. They were performing together at a music club in Norristown, Pennsylvania. They became immediate friends. Nelson asked Ted to go on tour with him and another life-long relationship was forged. Ted Paxson became Nelson's friend and accompanist for the remainder of Nelson's life, a total of thirty-seven years.

Singers, like politicians, often find themselves without honor in their own cities, but not Nelson. All of Nelson's old newspaper friends were now writing press articles about him. He sang for churches, banquets, musical teas, motion picture theaters and radio. Edouard Lippe was with him everyday.

"The Evening Bulletin" stated, "Nelson Eddy proved that he is capable of holding his own and keeping the audience thoroughly interested throughout, his voice retaining all of the luscious quality and authority of a real artist." And other snatches of print offered, "Nelson Eddy possesses none of the crudeness or uncertainty of the amateur." So it was that he made his first professional operatic debut with the Philadelphia Civic Opera Company in his appearance at the New York Metropolitan singing Tonio in "Pagliacci". Years later, the press agents exploited that Metropolitan appearance intimating that he had been a member of that renowned company. For the next five years he earned a reputation as a talented concert baritone and popular radio star. He paid back, in full, the bank loan with a sincere note of thanks.

Nelson was an ardent disciple of Feodor Ivanovitch Chaliapin, the Russian opera singer. They were very similar in background, talent, style and philosophy. Chaliapin like Nelson was self taught, a book lover who was always inclined toward the aesthetic arts. He was most famous in

America for his portrayal of "Boris Godunof". Nelson, a serious singer, loved to sing "Godunof".

The comparisons between the two are intriguing and astonishing. Nelson believed himself to be a teller of stories in song as did Chaliapin. In appearance, both were blond, blue-eyed and tall. Chaliapin was described as "a blond giant with the smiling face of a radiantly happy boy." Both had a flair for the humorous and both maintained an expansive naturalness and friendliness throughout their lives. Chaliapin was one of Nelson's ideals. He included many of Chaliapin's songs in his concert repertoire such as the *Volga Boatman, The Moon is High, Do Not Weep My Child, The Miller* and *Song of the Flea.* Nelson's recorded version of these songs are eloquent. If one could find a collector's recording of Chaliapin and Nelson to compare the voices, one would find a striking resemblance.

The country was in the throes of the stock market crash and nothing was ever to be the same. Old and firmly entrenched stars no longer wanted to sing for the Depression pay offered on the concert tours. Tickets were sold for 55 cents, 85 cents or $1.10 with the most expensive concert ticket being $2.75. Opportunities were afforded to young singers such as Nelson and he was ready and eager to step in with determination and fortitude. He knew it was more important that the world know him rather than pay him. People packed the halls and filled chairs along the side aisles---even on the stage itself! His heart told him to sing and forget the Depression, so he sang his heart out to the people who needed his music to brighten what had become a bleak world. In return, their appreciation took the form of curtain call after curtain call. Nelson became known as a "Depression Star"....he was on his way!

Often times his concerts would take him back to Rhode Island. The hometown newspapers were happy to write about Nelson. One newspaper wrote, "Among the generation that remembered the young Nelson much more clearly are his great aunts on the Eddy side". All the Eddys would come to his concerts and, after his performance, would rush back stage to envelope him with love and praise. The relatives followed his career carefully, from the time of his youthful singing of church solos to his mastery of the trap drums. Providence also remembered how the Eddy family had been prominent in operettas and other musical entertainments during their ten years of residence in the city. Active correspondence was also kept up between Isabel and her relatives in New Bedford. Wherever Nelson and Isabel traveled, relatives and friends would gather. New Bedford hadn't seen Nelson since he was twelve years old. Though their recollections were rather hazy, they came in droves to see and hear their handsome fair-haired boy destined for musical fame. How that town loved its home-grown boy!

Nelson's sister Ginny remembers visiting Nelson as a young child:

> It was usually in the hotel where he was staying while giving a concert in New York, Boston, or close by. The visits were always brief. He would walk us to the elevators where we would say our goodbyes. It was too difficult for him to appear in public in those days. But, the best times were when he visited us in Jamestown or Pawtucket while our grandparents were still alive. It was always hard on my father to say good-bye. To Dad---the sun rose and set on Nelson.

In the years since Nelson's birth, America had experienced many great changes which affected our economy, influenced our culture and enhanced our lifestyles. The invention of new mechanical and electronic devices such as the phonograph, automobile and the radio were exposing millions of people to a whole new world of pleasure. It was an exciting time for would be "stars" because there were new avenues of opportunity available where their talents could be seen and heard.

Nelson grew up with radio. While radio was still in its experimental stages, he sang night after night on station WCAU in Philadelphia for free and began to attract a small audience. When he hit the airwaves in 1932, his program, "The Contented Hour" was sponsored by Hoffman Beverages. He always began the program by singing, "To you and to you, my friends ever true" from *Auld Lang Syne* in his beautiful baritone. After only one week on the air, the female population sat up and began to take notice. He was to remain on the radio doing various programs for the next twenty-two years. However, this first taste of notoriety across the airwaves was to cause Nelson great consternation.

The funny thing about Nelson was his uncanny ability to attract women without even trying. They didn't wait until he became famous to pursue him. They discovered Nelson long before the movie producers ever heard of him.

While he was singing on the local radio station back in Philadelphia, in his half-advertising, half-singing days, the first woman glued herself to his trail. She was a young romantic and, at first, it appeared she just wanted to wish him well. Nelson, being the kind and well-mannered young man he was, willingly obliged. He didn't receive many letters in those days and would always personally answer his fan mail. He sent off a short response saying that he appreciated her letter of encouragement. As the story goes, he asked if she had any requests. He also wrote practically the same letter to about two-hundred other fans.

However, this particular woman, who we'll call Ms. H., had the romantic inclination to take it personally. When

Nelson sang, at her suggestion, *Ah Sweet Mystery of Life,* he received another note from her with even stronger language. Though inexperienced, he sensed trouble was close at hand. Letter after letter came, until the fourth week, when he received nothing more from her. With great naivete, he put the letters away---to him it was finished business. However, she resumed writing, wanting to know if he was mad at her. Now she began to include peace offerings, trinkets and embroidered handkerchiefs.

Unfortunately, Nelson made the mistake of singing *Ah Sweet Mystery of Life* again on his program and there was our Ms. H. arriving by taxi just as Nelson was leaving the studio. She screamed, "Nelson, you have forgiven me...you sang our song tonight!", and her enraptured face told the story. She had taken the whole thing personally. Nelson took one look at her expression, picked up his heels and ran!

This was to become a continuing saga in Nelson's life and should have been a warning to him of what was to come. Maybe he would lose track of Ms. H., but where she left off, thousands of others would pick up. There were women everywhere. The trains had to be checked because Nelson would be mobbed and badgered by the fans. Hidden in hallways, dressing rooms, wherever he went, women swooned. Always immaculately attired, his red hair had now turned to light blond and his tall sturdy build resembled that of a football player. Oh, he knew he was good looking alright, but failed to recognize that it was the combination of his voice and good looks which drew the women to him.

There were many such stories which followed the same pattern. A new American disease spread across the nation, borne of frustrations, fixations and love sick women weaving dreams to the magic of his golden voice. They were overcome with "Nelson Eddy Madness". It grew to great proportions after Nelson made "Naughty Marietta" and it was to exact a high price from his very being.

In 1934, still an unknown, he sang Wolfram in "Tannhauser" with the San Francisco Opera. After his performance, the critics claimed for him a place among America's finest baritone's such as Lawrence Tibbett, Richard Bonelli and John Charles Thomas.

Nelson loved the Wagnerian roles best. He is credited with using a vocal technique which produced the "helden or heroic" sound. It's an overlooked technique and seldom used today. Lawrence Tibbett also utilized this method, but it was Nelson Eddy who perfected it. By 1932, he had learned to sing in French, Italian, Spanish, Russian and Yiddish.

However, opera was not to claim Nelson for its own; his films, concerts and radio schedules would capture more and more of his time. In truth, Nelson succumbed to an inner struggle about his own capabilities. He believed his voice was not strong enough to meet the demands of formal opera so he ultimately allowed his most fervent desire to fade quietly into the background.

It was the concert stage that thrilled Nelson. As he continued to travel the concert circuit, word spread across the country that this talented young man possessed something special. His effect on audiences was electrifying and the critics began to take notice. They wrote about him in terms of his personal physique as well as his glorious baritone voice. Words such as "bathed and scrubbed masculinity" and "virile muscular presence" became commonly used phrases in his reviews. The Kansas City Star captioned their review of Nelson's concert quite aptly: "Mr. Eddy hung up a boot when nature played Santa Claus."

All work and no play might have made Nelson a dull boy, but he strived to keep a balance in his life. It's true that the hard work and strife tended to overshadow the balance at times, but it would never last long. His humor and ability to laugh at himself often saved the day. Equally inbred with his ability for introspection and seriousness were the natural instincts of a born clown. His friends knew that a burst of song or a clever practical joke weren't far away as Nelson was an irrepressible comedian and mimic. He socialized with women but showed little interest in romancing anyone special.

It's the Spring of 1933, the Los Angeles music season is just beginning. Lotte Lehmann, the German born opera star is scheduled to perform. Reservations were made early, since Hollywood was always given advance notice of every accredited musical event. The night is filled with the power and glitter of Hollywood...the audience sparkling with diamonds and attired smartly in tuxedos and furs.

Nelson is on a concert tour on the West Coast and scheduled to perform that very same evening for the San Diego Philharmonic. He and Ted had already toured most of the country and his repertoire had grown to over 500 songs. He is totally unaware of the glamourous and powerful setting in Los Angeles. An emergency arises when Lotte Lehmann is suddenly taken ill, and an urgent phone call is placed to Nelson requesting that he take her place. This phone call and the following events will change Nelson's life forever.

Arrangements are made, and a rushed Nelson is hurriedly flown to Los Angeles. There is no time for him to prepare for the performance. Totally an unknown on the West Coast, Nelson, resolute, walks onto the stage. Thoroughly engaging and unaffected, he unleashes his brilliant baritone and the audience is enraptured. It's a brilliant success! Nelson responded to eighteen encores and many curtains call. Seldom had he experienced such an enthusiastic audience and seldom had an audience been so moved by a performance. Nelson was gracious, masculine and gentlemanly. The audience felt these qualities and perceived him as someone special.

Among the audience that night was Ida Koverman---the first-class helper of Louis B. Mayer, boss of MGM studios. Ida, known as his jack-of-all-trades, was his private secretary. She carried a lot of weight with Mayer.

Nelson was unaware of his profound effect on the audience. He sang with natural ease mainly because it was his calling. At thirty-two years of age, Nelson had grown very comfortable with himself. What people saw was a distinctive personality with a genuineness that was rare. What made Nelson unique was that he truly sang for the pure joy of singing. His interest in music was so much a part of his soul, there was no way to hide it. Nelson himself had said many times that "If people are not born with music in their souls, they should not try to sing. But if they are born with it, nothing in the world can keep them from singing." He was so rightly fitted into his world, so wondrously honed and tuned to deliver such perfect harmony. One had to smile at such perfection.

Nelson would have sung whatever his occupation might have been. He had made the necessary sacrifices and carved out a secure place for his talents. However, he never dreamed his career would take him to Hollywood. He certainly was never groomed for stardom...he was an oratorio singer, and his home was the concert stage.

Chapter Five

Ida Koverman went immediately to her boss and raved about the talented singer. When she presented him to Louis B. Mayer, she was perceptive enough to present a total view of him which encompassed his good looks, his genuineness and his beautiful voice. She demanded and got a screen test for Nelson.

Hollywood in the 30's was indeed a magical kingdom made up of kings and queens, along with the squires and soldiers needed to protect them. The aura that surrounded that "Golden Era of Entertainment" is recaptured for us today with the resurgence of old nostalgia and memorabilia.

Hollywood then was a place where bosses were bosses, stars were stars. It was a unique community where people fought hard, played hard and worked together for one sole purpose---to make movies. The studios felt that the musical comedy operettas had run their course by then. The general conception of the studio bosses was that the public was ready for good solid heroes and heroines. They wanted no more imaginary characters singing their stories to each other.

This is the Hollywood Nelson enters. The studio called the day after his concert. An unknown voice asked, "Mr. Eddy, could you report to the Culver City Plant at your earliest convenience for a screen test? If you photograph well" the studio implied, "we might give you a contract." And Nelson replied, "I'm not sure I want one". How can this be---anyone would almost kill for a chance at stardom. Anyone but Nelson, that is.

Nelson's side of the story about signing the contract is as follows:

> When I came to Los Angeles about a year ago, I had no thought of pictures. I was on a regular concert tour, and when MGM offered me a contract, nobody was more surprised than I. I didn't truly know whether to sign or not, but while I was trying to think it over, my agent practically did it for me.

That's not entirely true; Nelson had weighed his options carefully. The film and recording industries enticed him. Talking pictures were only five years old and new inventions were already on the horizon. Bill encouraged Nelson to see the opportunity before him. Both father and son were fascinated by electronic devices and gadgets.

It should be noted that RKO Studios was also interested in him, but they were suffering financial problems at the time. Even though they were interested in signing Nelson, the best they could offer him was half the amount that MGM was offering. MGM was in fact cutting the salaries of many stars because of the Depression, yet Nelson was lured to sign what many described as a more lucrative contract. In comparison to RKO, it was a good offer. If Nelson was to enter uncharted territory, he would not go alone. Lippe, Ted Paxson and Isabel Eddy were right by his side and would remain so. Ted Paxson had recently married. He and his new bride stayed with Isabel and Nelson until they could find a place of their own. Helen Paxson became Nelson's first secretary.

When Nelson finally signed, it didn't take him long to discover that he had made a terrible mistake. The original contract not only would keep him idle, but it would prevent him from doing what he really loved to do, which was concertize. He took one look at the sound stage, the impersonal trappings and the pretense of the stars and was sick at heart. He was already uneasy in his new surroundings---this just made it worse. Luckily, the Yankee part of him took over.

After he signed the contract, he discovered he had no parts. Little as he cared for Hollywood, he couldn't just sit there. Logical, analytical and purposeful of mind, he began to think relentlessly of what he should do. He sorely missed the warm responses of a live audience. His body demanded him to work; his mind demanded him to work; his soul cried out for some effort. Here he was....presented with the first chance to rest in his life, a chance to just sit in the old easy chair and he couldn't bring himself to buy one moment of it. Idleness and nonsense are attributes he neither favored nor respected. He filled his waking hours with a new interest---acting. He nosed around the studio asking questions, investigating the sound equipment and cameras. Once again, he felt challenged. He continued to improve his singing, concentrating on the sound and range of his voice.

It's important to recognize how Nelson had lived for the past ten years of his life. Months of overnight travel, crushing crowds, rehearsals and performances every night, signing autographs, squeezing in radio broadcasts, answering mail, trying to catch an hour or two of sleep here and there. It would be very difficult for any one of us to develop that pace, but even harder would be our adjustment---should it simply stop. Add in the fact that, being a perfectionist, he gave more of himself to please his public than most entertainers of that time.

As early as August of 1932, he had fainted during a broadcast in New York because of the close heat. One really has to stop and question the reason why someone as robust and healthy as Nelson collapses simply from exhaustion. It is very obvious that he was pushing himself far past the norm. Were he here today, he would tell us that it was because of his passion and drive. He would also admit he was a workaholic. Take away his passion, his need to strive, and you have an idea of Nelson's first year in Hollywood.

The signs were there and Nelson fell apart. Rarely ill, he got a very bad cold and admitted to being depressed; his depression was something he found absolutely unfathomable. Nelson was so desperate that he would come over to the studio in the morning all dressed up and sit around. Producers would walk by him and ask, "What are you doing here so early in the morning?" Nelson would reply, "Why, I'm waiting to be called on the set." One producer just laughed at him and suggested, "Oh, Nelson, go out and play some golf. We'll give you a ring when we need you. There isn't a story for you yet." Nelson resolved one day to be a good soldier and take the producer's advice. He didn't want to play golf, but he had to shake himself.

Nelson became very cynical during this time of anxiety and was the first to admit it. Moody and filled with self recrimination, he saw no way out.

> After my return from abroad, my singing netted me about $3,000 the first year; $6,000 the second; and after a while, I was making from $16,000 to $30,000 a year. So when I went into films I knew I could sing, but I had grave doubts about possessing a picture personality. Having signed the contract, I would report for work and there would be nothing. Nothing happened; nobody knew I lived, breathed or sang a note. After a week I toned down my arrival to 9:30 a.m.; still nothing happened, nobody saw me, noticed me or heard me. Thank goodness for that producer

> that told me to go do something practical and worthwhile with my time.

Nelson and Isabel had settled into a small home in California. Isabel made friends quickly and enjoyed the feeling of being settled into a permanent home once again. To nourish his interests and occupy his time, Nelson began to create a recording apparatus which cluttered up most of the living room. It turned out to be a most ingenious invention. He would practice new songs and replay the recordings while taking fastidious notes on where improvement was needed. Nelson even used his recorder to play practical jokes on his friends. Later he would rehearse his spoken lines and play them back for effect. Isabel tried in vain to get him to move the whole setup out of the living room, but to no avail.

In 1933, Louis B. Mayer was the highest paid man in America. His salary was $1.2 million. The rewritten contract Nelson and Mayer signed called for Nelson to give exclusive services to MGM for seven years. But Nelson was smart enough to also include a provision that allowed him to take three months of every year to continue his concertizing. This new contract saved his sanity. No matter how demanding his film roles became, they were never allowed to interfere with his annual concerts.

Once again, fate was on hand to provide an opportunity. Nelson by now was at his wit's end. He was impatient, anxious and frustrated because nothing was happening. An actor named Gene Molin was chosen to sing the song *Rhythm of the Day* in the finale of the movie "Dancing Lady" which starred Joan Crawford and Clark Gable. "Dancing Lady" was also the screen debut of Fred Astaire. However, Gene was seriously injured in a car accident and was unable to perform his song. Rather than wait for him to recover, the studio was anxious to find someone just Gene's size as a replacement, so he could fit into his wardrobe, thereby saving the studio money. Nelson Eddy was just the right size! After two years of waiting, Nelson had his first assignment. He sang the song, but he was terribly uncomfortable. He was not used to working without an audience and he had never before had to synchronize his songs to match his lip movements. In his first screen debut, he not only appeared stiff to others, he felt it within himself.

To make matters worse, MGM did not release the film on time. Many articles later suggested that "Broadway to Hollywood", made in 1933, was his first film. However, that is incorrect. When Nelson did see himself on the screen, it only increased his anxiety. "It didn't take me very long to sing my part and, again, I was in the dog house and on the loose," he bemoaned. "It didn't look as if Nelson Eddy was going to get very far in the picture business at all."

Ted Paxson finally got into the act in "Broadway to Hollywood" with Frank Morgan and Alice Brady. When Nelson sang the concert number, Ted accompanied him on the piano. Nelson's next screen appearance was in "Student Tour" starring Jimmy Durante in 1934. Nelson had a small part playing himself and singing *The Carlo,* a new dance rhythm in five-four time which was supposed to strike a blow to jazz. After "Student Tour" he was so upset with his screen image that he went to Mayer and asked to be released from his contract. Louis B. placated him by saying all he needed was the right script, the right director, the right co-star and acting lessons. If Nelson could have had his way, he would have broken the contract right then and there.

Louis B. Mayer was known to hate blond actors, but Nelson was the exception for several reasons. Nelson's personality, voice, good looks and dedication sold him right from the start. But something else was happening to cause Louis B. to placate Nelson. Fan mail was beginning to pour in. "Who was that luscious baritone with the beautiful voice?" the letters asked.

When a film was previewed by the theaters, they would pass out post cards to the audience on which to write their reactions. When "Dancing Lady" and "Broadway to Hollywood" were previewed, the same queries came back. "Who is the man who sang the song?" He had amassed only seven minutes of screen time---yet his magnetism was already drawing attention. Since he received his life's breath from the public, Nelson had become a true transmitter. Whenever he sang, not only his beautiful voice, but his love for singing spread an emotional warmth over all he touched. Now this warmth was being transmitted onto the motion picture screen.

Nelson was still scared. He really didn't fit into the Hollywood lifestyle. He felt that he could give his all to motion pictures just as he had done in his concerts, but it would never work. He was suffocating in Hollywood. He said, "A thing you build your life on doesn't die in three years. Singing is my life." Yet, in the back of his mind was the realization that by using the medium of film, he could sing to millions.

Nelson loved his practical jokes and they saved his sanity in many ways. One time he visited the home of a friend who was on the staff of MGM and instead of announcing himself by name, he sang an aria from "Rigoletto" which won him considerable applause from all the neighbors.

Where was his private life? Where were all the women? Nelson had many friends, those who met him instinctively liked him. He entertained his friends with teas and parties in his home. In fact, the press comments on

Nelson were always very favorable. His personality, appearance, sense of well-being, naivete and generosity all contributed to his star quality. Louella Parsons knew a winner when she saw one. She lived near Nelson and took great interest in his comings and goings. His first public gossip was written by Louella---a one liner that read, "Nelson Eddy gets a speeding ticket." She never missed writing about Nelson's parties. After one particular party she wrote, "Nelson entertained more than 100 guests Sunday afternoon, November 5th, at a cocktail party in his home. He used his phonograph machine to become a one-man quartet." Louella also wasted no time in finding a romance for Nelson. He was linked with Lila Lee as early as 1933.

Nelson respected people who put effort into their careers and didn't have time for the "Hollywood syndrome". Off the set, he liked to pal around with Clark Gable and Robert Taylor as well as his old friends. Clark and Robert were as down to earth as Nelson. They had some good times together. What his close friends knew was that Nelson was the breath of life of many parties. His imitation of Greta Garbo making her farewell scene in "Queen Christina" was the talk of Hollywood. They hung out at a little speakeasy called Pete's at 49th and 1st Avenue with a group of friends. It was the kind of place where beer was spilled on the counter and a few drunks would reel around the room. Nelson willingly sang requests for patrons who never knew who he really was. His friends claimed he was the best impromptu story teller in song---he was a raconteur; his talent competed with the best vaudeville acts of the time. He told stories in Russian, Dutch or Irish dialect, many of which were bawdy as well as humorous. In later years, he would have loved to have gone back to Pete's just to be himself again.

When Nelson met Hollywood and his star began to rise, there were expectations of him to go "Hollywood". His "yankee levelheadedness" proved stronger than the environment in which he now lived, and it brought the reporters to their knees. Reporters want news stories and stars thrive on publicity---not Nelson. From the moment he entered "moviedom" he made it very clear that his private life was private. "Just wait. He'll catch on," they said. "He'll change his mode of living, even his disposition." Incredible as it may seem, the world found out very quickly that Nelson meant every word; he refused to go "Hollywood". Stars spend a great deal of time worrying about their image, they put the emphasis on their bodies, clothes, makeup and cars. Nelson put his emphasis on his inner qualities. He knew he owed much to the thousands of fans who came to his concerts, and being conscientious to a fault, he held firm to his own true self and the very qualities that made his fans love him. He had come to Hollywood as the most popular and sought after concert singer of his time. He trusted his own instincts and his public trusted him.

The dilemma remained---what to do with Nelson Eddy? Even Hunt Stromberg, the producer, couldn't answer the question. He was convinced that MGM had a great find but he was also convinced that it would take a particular type of role to put him over. None of the films on the MGM schedule contained such a role. When Nelson did sing in "Dancing Lady", it was just to give him experience. Nelson was always proud of the fact that while he was waiting for some type of opportunity to prove whether or not he was a good screen bet, he learned 30 new songs, two complete operas and very nearly mastered the Russian language. In off hours, he used up nervous energy by immersing himself in horseback riding, golf or tennis. All of his life, Nelson exercised in some form. His first love had been swimming, but a reoccurring eye infection caused him to give it up. He wasn't one to baby himself in anyway. He ate and drank what he liked; he smoked both a pipe and cigarettes; he drank occasionally; and never took any special precautions with his voice.

The fan mail grew, and by now the women in Hollywood were becoming infatuated as well. One look at his clear blue eyes and powerful frame and the starlets began their pursuit. Nelson took a good look at these women and was not happy with what he saw. He didn't like silly or giddy women. He liked a woman of substance and depth. To make matters worse, he was shy around women and unknowledgable about them. The demands of his career had left him a bit lopsided in this area. Instinctively, he felt Hollywood was not the kind of place where he could find his ideal woman.

Chapter Six

Jeanette MacDonald was a lead star on the MGM lot. She was considered a heavy weight having already starred in five leading roles. Jeanette knew how to steel herself against the over zealous fans, the hanger-ons and the back stabbers. Her years in Hollywood had helped her develop the defenses necessary for survival. She was a professional in every sense of the word and her vast knowledge about lighting, sound, makeup and wardrobe was unmatched.

Irving Thalberg, the famous producer, was convinced that 1933 was the year to renew the cycle of the song and dance films. Proof of that was Warner Brother's lavish "42nd Street" which was an expansive production and had done quite well. Around the MGM lot, awareness that the musical operetta might make a come back caused quite a stir. But "Naughty Marietta" was not an extravaganza, it was to be a low budget type "A" film. "Naughty Marietta" was a favorite of Mayers, and it had been on hold for quite some time.

The story goes that Allan Jones was originally offered the lead, but Jones was under contract to the Shuberts at that time. The Shuberts wanted $50,000 for his release. Jones, put in a very difficult position, asked friends if they might lend him the money. MGM, not wanting legal entanglements with the Shuberts and hearing nothing from Jones, stopped the negotiations. The studio assumed incorrectly that Allan Jones' efforts had failed and offered Nelson the male lead. Actually, Jeanette is said to have had some choice in the matter as well as Nelson's fan, Ida Koverman. Jeanette and Nelson had been suggested as a team for the musical version of "The Prisoner of Zenda", but the movie never materialized. By the time Allan Jones checked in with Mayer, it was too late. Fate took its course once again as Jeanette MacDonald and Nelson Eddy were paired together to become the most popular singing team of all time.

By the time "Naughty Marietta" became a reality, Nelson and Jeanette were inspiring each other. According to the gossip mill they even dated. Research shows that these were not dates. They were "get togethers" for the sole purpose of sharing common goals, ideas and friendship. Jeanette shared with Nelson her knowledge of Hollywood. After all, "Naughty Marietta" would be her thirteenth film. She explained to him about the image of stardom, while Nelson was inspiring Jeanette to reach for more serious singing, as opera had always been her dream.

Louis B. Mayer wasted no time in priming Jeanette. She was gracious enough to share equal billing with Nelson, an unknown, and Mayer wanted to make sure something was in it for her. He told her that the role in "Naughty Marietta" would give her a wider emotional range in her singing and she shouldn't be afraid to put her heart into her voice. Jeanette felt her career was faltering a bit since her Maurice Chevalier musicals and she had high hopes for "Naughty Marietta".

Nelson, on the other hand, felt little of the confidence that Jeanette possessed. Nelson brought along Dr. Lippe who became his voice coach, film coach, and all around coach, on to the set. In fact, Lippe even got a bit part as the innkeeper. Poor Nelson was terrified. He knew the movements of opera acting, but this was his first attempt at screen acting. Hunt Stromberg had warned Louis B. Mayer that the picture's main song *Ah, Sweet Mystery of Life* was also the Forest Lawn Cemetery theme song. It could make or break the film. Nelson carried the additional burden of delivering the song in a way that would sell the song and not the cemetery.

The director, W.S. Van Dyke was known on the lot as "one take" Van Dyke. He had successfully directed Myrna Loy and William Powell in the "Thin Man" and was riding high on the critic's acclaim. He was about to create the cinematic image of the world's perfectly matched sweethearts, but his immediate problem was Nelson.

Woody knew he had a neophyte on his hands. Nelson found it very difficult to lip sync, so Van Dyke decided to let him record his songs in the recording studio with full orchestra rather than in front of the camera. This compromise probably saved Nelson's career. He later became more comfortable with lip syncing and could handle it quite well on his own.

There were other problems to eliminate. Thank goodness Van Dyke was a prankster like Nelson. It was through his jokes that he loosened up the cast so that their natural feelings came through. At one point, Nelson kept missing a high note and all the musicians were glaring at him. The next time Nelson tried to hit the fatal note, Van Dyke blasted sirens at the same time---every one laughed including Nelson. The prank loosened Nelson up and the next try was perfect.

The making of "Naughty Marietta" turned out to be an enjoyable experience for Jeanette, Nelson and Van Dyke. They had fun together. In one take, Nelson accidentally ran into a tree because he wasn't watching where he was going. Laughing at himself, Nelson asked Van Dyke to leave it in the film.

When it came time for the preview of "Naughty Marietta", they both shared a strong case of the jitters. How the public viewed the picture would decide their individual futures. After the preview of "Naughty Marietta", to which only the select were invited, Hollywood proclaimed that an exciting new star had arisen. "Naughty Marietta" won the Movie of the Year Award in "Photoplay" magazine. It made Nelson an overnight success.

His radio fans answered, "That star has been shining in the radio heavens for ages." Although Nelson is primarily remembered for his roles in the frothy operettas, anyone who lived in Philadelphia or heard Nelson in concert during the 1920's cannot forget what a fine opera singer he was. Jeanette also became a new star with a new personality. They had no idea they would eventually complete the most successful film operettas in screen history.

After the release of the film, everyone was apparently more excited than Nelson. He tersely announced that he was the same Nelson Eddy he was last week or last month and his voice was not one bit different than last week when he sang his favorite song on the air for radio fans. After his overnight success, he still had grave doubts. His voice is what brought him the dividends. When on a tour, he would give one hundred and fifty per cent of himself. There wasn't an evening that didn't go by when he wasn't trying out a new song or changing part of a program. He would study scores during breakfast and iron out problems with stage managers, orchestra arrangers and conductors. Without the concertizing and weekly radio programs, Nelson was deprived of two necessities: his craving for a live audience and his primary source of income. The truth is that Nelson was paid very little by MGM for his movies. The film colony knew it---all of Hollywood knew it. Nelson was a concert singer who made films, not a film star who gave concerts.

It was still the Depression decade and the public went to the movies to forget. For a quarter at the matinee or a dime in the back of the house, a housewife could purchase something that was unattainable anywhere else in her life. She could buy escape for a small price. Because women were the movie going majority, they were the ones who shopped for their dreams and the glamor that was so sadly lacking in their real lives. They bought the fair-haired hero with the blue eyes and wonderful smile. They loved the appealing and vivacious heroine; they loved "the team" and they clamored for more. The operettas were set in the past; the plots took place in mythical locations in far away kingdoms alive with beautiful costumes and the romantic music of Victor Herbert, Sigmund Romberg, Rudolph Friml and even Cole Porter.

It wasn't the musical fantasies that caused such an uproar; it was the blending of two perfect voices and the union of their talents. The chemistry was undeniable. "Naughty Marietta" remains one of the top box office draws in the history of motion pictures. The movie made the studio's head spin. They had struck gold but didn't realize the depth of their strike, because Nelson Eddy was immediately scheduled to play opposite Grace Moore in Rudolph Friml's "Rose Marie". Fortunately for the world, Grace rejected the role for two reasons. Her schedule offered little time to prepare for the movie and Nelson, an unknown, was not important enough to cause her to adjust her busy schedule. MGM then cast Jeanette opposite Nelson for the second time, still not completely aware of the impact "the team" had on the public.

If Nelson thought he had girl problems before the release of "Naughty Marietta", they grew a thousand fold after the public saw the movie. He was always being linked with some starlet in Hollywood. He was supposedly smitten by Cecilia Parker in 1934. Yet he remained extremely private, never giving out any information of his own accord. His reclusive attitude caused Hollywood gossips to hint that his obvious masculine charms covered deeper secrets. What kind of a man lives with his mother and refuses to openly date, they whispered. Nelson was well aware of these rumors, reacting privately with varying degrees of anguish, but to the press, he remained mute. He stubbornly refused to date glamor girls just to appease the Hollywood rumor mill. Nelson's only comment about his love life: "I keep it all to myself...it's a closed book."

Up until this point in time, he had managed to untangle himself from the rumors of his romantic dalliances. Nelson had very firm expectations of what marriage entailed. His chances of settling down seemed less and less as commitments left little time for the social scene. Women in turn began to wonder if they could hold on to the number one box office star, or would they want to, considering the hardships and pressures of his status.

Nelson questioned the very same things. There were certain attributes that he respected in women. He disliked giddiness, and self-affected females left him cold. Only a very special type of woman could ever marry a man such as Nelson Eddy. She would have to possess tremendous strength and self esteem in her own right. Nelson didn't believe that people in the same profession should marry. He felt there would be jealousy---that it couldn't be helped. He abhorred competition within marriage as he had seen many of his friends' marriages fail. Having been the victim of a broken marriage himself, he was not about to take any unnecessary risks. He realized that a wife would either be a big help to him or a great interference.

He was looking for a woman whose ego did not demand her to compete with him, but rather to assist him. He knew what was right for him, it's just that he privately doubted he would ever find such a person. Cultured, well read, possessing substance and depth yet gracious and unassuming; these were important qualities to him. Finding a mate was not an issue he chose to discuss openly, since those close to him knew his desires. Besides, life was bountiful and good to him. He had his friends, his fans and his family, and above all, his talent to keep him happy.

Nelson and Gene Raymond were good friends. They were the only two blond leading men in the business in 1934. They were also avid tennis rivals and played together quite often. By 1934, Nelson had already established himself as one of the best dressed men in Hollywood. He held that distinction for several years with Ronald Colman and George Brent.

For the next few years, Nelson was forced to change his phone number weekly and had to install an iron grill door for protection. What an adjustment for someone who loved freedom; he was forced into a far more secluded lifestyle. Hollywood needed a romance for their star, and the fan magazines hit the news stands proclaiming Alice Faye was his latest true love. I talked with Alice while she was visiting Chicago recently. She asked me to clear up the romance rumor once and for all:

"Nelson took me to lunch only once and all I could do was stare at him---he was so handsome. I never saw him again after our lunch. I wish I could have claimed this hot romance. He was a wonderful man."

Bevies of beautiful girls clustered around him at this point in his life; he was overwhelmed. As he put it so aptly:

> It's a topsy-turvy world. Two days ago nobody in Hollywood knew or cared whether I lived or didn't. Today the place is literally swarming with people who seemed to be vitally and personally concerned with my welfare. All because I sang songs similar to others that I have been singing over the radio for years. And

> incidently, I didn't sing them any better than I have dozens of times before. Everybody from the newspapers and magazines offers me the same advice. It frightens me. They entreat me not to let my success go to my head. They ask me not to go Hollywood, whatever that is. It almost takes the fun out of the whole thing. When I came to Los Angeles several years ago, I was Nelson Eddy the singer and I am the same Nelson Eddy today.

Although he bought a new home, he resisted fancy cars and flamboyant clothes. He shied away from the Hollywood scene. He was often forced to lock himself behind the grilled gates and he spent his time developing one of the finest privately owned musical libraries in the world. He continued to add new scores, sheet music and musical literature to the library, personally cataloging the entire collection. He was named the top singer of operatic and classical songs by Radio Guide Magazine's "Star Poll" in 1936.

To Isabel, Nelson was still and always would be the ideal son. His mother should know best and she said so often. Others confirmed the title. Nelson was caring, respectful and loving. Isabel always referred to her son as "Nelse" and he called her "Muz". Many Hollywood reports publicized the mother and son association with lack of depth and sincerity. This hurt Nelson a great deal. Nelson remained utterly adamant all his life in refusing to allow publicity to enter his private life. Much of what was written in those days was manufactured publicity and was very often quite harmful and untrue. That's why it's important that, after much research and talking with the family, the association of Nelson and his mother be depicted more clearly. There is absolutely nothing about Nelson and his mother or his friends that smacked of Hollywood. Nelson and his mother had fun together; they were respectful of each other, very protective and equal friends. Parents and friends intermingled. Included in Nelson's cadre of friends were Ted and Helen Paxson and Dr. Lippe. Ginny remembers her father visited Nelson quite often. She recalls her relationship with Nelson during those early years:

> I was rather a brat to him when I was young. He was talented, handsome and famous and I was this skinny tom-boy. I remember acting up in his presence to get attention and any attention was better than none at all. I use to call him a "yellow-haired cricket tail", the cricket tails referred to the formal tails he wore for concerts. I think he could have clobbered me to a wall, really, and I know my parents did reprimand me. We weren't close in the early years since we were twenty-five years apart. It wasn't until the later years that we drew closer together.

Isabel was romantically linked with Lippe for quite some time, and it was thought that she would marry before Nelson. There were no wedding bells, but Isabel and Lippe always remained good friends.

Isabel had started a scrap book for Nelson back in 1921. She proudly cut and pasted every picture and article into the book. Friends who visited their home remember Isabel dragging around this perfectly enormous scrap book of her "Nelse". If there ever was a work of love---this was one. In the years to follow there would be many more scrapbooks to fill. I had the pleasure of researching these scrapbooks. Isabel carefully wrote these words on the front page of the first scrapbook, "This is not for beauty, but for reference---with love."

Before his move to Hollywood, Nelson had been a nomad; he was used to constant travel---a new bed every night. He felt that being a nomad was in his genes, instilled from his early beginnings. In later life, it would even become a characteristic of Isabel's. In Hollywood, however, he became scheduled. Up at 6:00 a.m., an avid tennis player, he would usually play six sets of tennis, then vocalize for hours, study foreign languages and work with his dialogue coach, Oliver Hinsdell.

Settled into a new home, other routines developed. A typical day for Nelson always included Ted and Lippe coming by in the morning. Nelson liked to sleep late, but always arrived downstairs fully clothed. No one ever saw Nelson in various stages of undress. Meticulous to a fault, his New England upbringing appeared in everything he did.

All he needed to complete his new image was a dog. He pictured a nice sleek little animal waiting anxiously for him at the door every night when he came home. Then Jeanette gave him Sheba as a gift. Sheba was a sheep dog, big as a horse, with hair constantly hanging in her eyes. She wasn't exactly what Nelson had envisioned, but she was a definite hit. The thing that always got to Nelson was that, when he finally did enter the house, Sheba never paid any attention to him. She just continued to sleep contentedly. Nelson adored her. Everyday he would romp with her as she followed him from room to room.

When Nelson felt happy and comfortable, he was a creative prankster. He loved to record all his parties and then play back the recordings. Everyone caught on to what he was doing, so at his parties they would interject spicy little tidbits. He was "infamous" for saving old Christmas cards, only to return them to the sender the following Christmas.

Thousands of letters came daily from his film admirers and thousands more came from his radio admirers. As Nelson prepared to make his next film, this favorite story summed up his feelings. When Woody Van Dyke met Nelson at the train after his overnight success in "Naughty Marietta", Woody asked, "How does it feel to be a star?" Nelson replied, "I don't know how to act". To which old Woody said, "You're telling me!" Nelson loved that story because it was so true. Nelson never pretended that he knew how to act. His charm on the screen emanated from the very fact that he couldn't act. We shared his trepidation and good humor as he tried. Away from the camera, Nelson loved to have fun. He was extremely popular with the publicity department. What really counted was that he was just as welcome with the girls in the publicity department before "Naughty Marietta" as well as after. He was always grateful for that.

Louella Parsons had a hot bit of gossip one day. Isabel was greatly distressed when Nelson received a threatening phone call. The caller announced that something of an "amazing nature" would befall him. The police were immediately notified, and a police guard was placed outside their home. At this time, he and Isabel were living at 619 N. Foothill Boulevard in Beverly Hills. Nelson did a little investigating and discovered that a number of well-known Hollywood residents had been recently threatened and terrorized. Nelson's old reporting skills were fast at work, much to the dismay of Isabel. After piecing together the facts, Nelson suspected a hoax. In cooperation with the police, he discovered a local detective agency had made the threatening calls, thinking it a very clever way to drum up new business. After placing the threatening phone call, the detective agency would offer the frightened victim a body guard. Pretty clever ruse---the police closed in and caught the culprits.

Chapter Seven

A most generous man, Nelson gave from his heart to friends and strangers alike. On his concert tours he would find time to encourage or help people in the most unexpected ways.

One of the more poignant stories involved a young singer whom Nelson met while on concert tour in Iowa. He had just enough time to attend a local production of "Carmen" and, on that particular evening, one of the town's local girls was making her debut in a leading role. Nelson, seated in the audience, recognized that she was very nervous and frightened. Her voice was affected by her troubled state of mind. The audience did nothing to help the uncomfortable situation; polite applause was almost worse than no applause at all. Nelson realized that, although the young singer had a lovely voice, her state of mental stress prevented her from bringing it out. After what seemed an interminably long time, the curtain came down.

Nelson, overcome with sympathy, went back stage after the final curtain only to be mobbed by admirers. When he finally got through to her dressing room, he discovered she had already gone home in tears. Nelson got her name and address and hailed a taxi. He had only forty minutes to make his next train. He found the house and quickly surmised that the family had not yet arrived home. Remembering his own periods of despair and how little he wanted to be around anyone during those times, he rang the bell and called out, "Western Union!" In a few moments she came to the door. While he tried to explain, she kept him out on the porch. He did not tell her his name, and she certainly didn't recognize him in the dark shadows. He told her he had heard her sing, "I think you have a beautiful voice, and I have studied a lot myself and I should know," he explained. "I have a suggestion. Leave this town when you can and start over again somewhere else, for if you are as sensitive as I think you are, you will have a hard time living down tonight, within yourself, I mean."

Suddenly the young woman became completely unnerved and began to sob. Nelson listened as all her anguished thoughts and feelings came tumbling out. She was hopeless---life was hopeless. Expressing sympathy, he told her of a man who had gone from one singing teacher to another and, after fifteen years of discouragement, had only begun to realize any success at all. For years this man had been singing wrong and not getting the best out of his voice. Time and time again people advised him to give it up. Then Nelson began to point out certain elements of her style and suggested how she could improve her singing. He offered to give her some breathing and vocalizing exercises that he had worked out. Convinced of his concern, she invited him in to use the piano. As the dim light reflected upon his features, she exclaimed, "You're Nelson Eddy, it was you you were talking about."

Nelson said, "Yes, but let's not waste time because I have to go." At that, he quickly showed her breathing exercises, and the startled and bewildered young woman followed along with him. Ten minutes later the family drove up just as Nelson was driving away. He called out over his shoulder, "If you come out to Hollywood, come and see me." That young woman did eventually go to Hollywood and studied as never before. Although she never attained stardom, her life was enriched by that eventful evening, and they stayed in touch for many years.

Nelson - 5 years old

Choir boy

Boyhood sketch

Nelson - 8 years old

Nelson, sitting on drum, with his father at Fort Greble - 1910

Pawtucket School Days - Nelson, fifth from left, bottom row

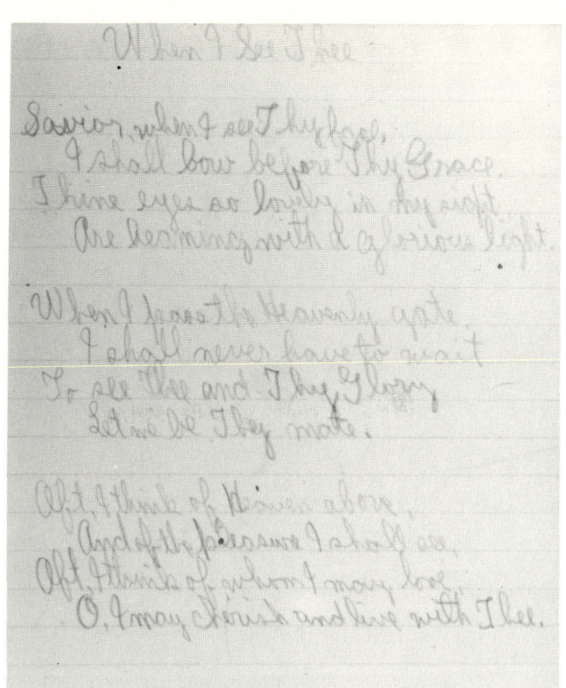

When I See Thee

Savior, when I see Thy face,
I shall bow before Thy Grace.
Thine eyes so lovely in my sight
Are beaming with a glorious light.

When I pass the Heavenly gate
I shall never have to wait
To see Thee and Thy Glory
Let me be Thy mate.

Oft, I think of Heaven above,
And of the pleasure I shall see,
Oft, I think of whom I may love,
O, I may cherish and live with Thee.

Poem written by Nelson in 5th grade

Church of the Savior, Philadelphia (Nelson in circle)

Nelson as a teenager

The Lenox,
13th and Spruce Streets,
Philadelphia, Pa.,
June 10, 1929

Roland L. Taylor

Dear Mr. Taylor:

It has been hard work, but I made It!

If you remember, I told you at the beginning of the season I aimed to make at least $5,000 this year.

For a while I was a little anxious about it, but a few unexpected dates came in and the total for the season is a little over $6,000.

I have had 75 engagements, as follows:

28	Concerts	$1,735.
11	Operas	800.
5	Recitals	650.
16	Radio	465.
5	Private Recitals	430.
4	Oratorios	250.
5	Special Church Services	195.
1	Week at Stanley Theatre	350.
		4,875.
	Overbrook Pres. Church	1,200.
		6,075.

I have definitely placed myself on a satisfactory living basis. All expenses have been paid. I have no outstanding bills. I have continued my monthly assistance to my Mother. And I have a few hundred dollars left with which to do something this Summer.

I am enclosing a check for $500., which is my first modest step in paying back the $8,000. you have loaned me. This is one of the happiest moments of my career, because it marks the turning point in my earning capacity, from loss toward profit. Another happy day will be when I will have paid all of it back to you.

I am going to aim at $10,000. next season. It is quite an order, but I will try hard. I will have my Church job ($1,200.) and I have signed a contract with the Civic Opera that probably will bring $1,000. (The opera will carry on for at least one more year, despite the 3½ million loss occasioned by the intestate death of Attmore Robinson.) I will have a dozen or more radio jobs on the Newton Coal Forum Hour and a few concert engagements already are taking shape for next year. So there is a start, at least.

I have not made Summer plans yet. When I do, I will talk them over with you.

Again I express my gratitude to you for helping me and I hppe that eventually I may make you feel that your kindness was fruitful.

Sincerely,

Roland L. Taylor
1421 Chestnut Street
Philadelphia

June 11, 1929

Mr. Nelson Eddy
The Lenox
13th and Spruce Streets
Philadelphia, Pa.

Dear Nelson:

I beg leave to acknowledge receipt of your letter of the 10th instant and feel that perhaps I am only a little less happy over your accomplishment than are you.

This is perhaps your most important milestone - To have started and made fair success in one profession and then to have deliberately abandoned that for a course of study in a totally different profession was a change which no doubt caused you much anxious thought and the responsibility for your future which meant either failure or success in life. Of course, had you failed in this you were young enough to start over again in something else but undoubtedly the enthusiasm of youth would have been very hard hit and your second start would have been very difficult. This year, therefore, I feel with you, is the turning point and should be a very good augury for a much greater success in the future.

The deaths of Mrs. Hilprecht and Mr. Robinson, I fear from what little I know, will be a very hard blow to Civic Opera, and the joining together of Mrs. Leidy's opera with the Bok School of Music ought to give them a tremendous advantage. My first impression is that the Civic Opera is going to have a very hard time to exist under these circumstances unless some new "angel" can be found.

For your sake I am glad you have been able to make the first payment on account of the cost of your musical education. Come in when you are ready or phone and make an appointment and I shall be glad to hear more of your plans.

Sincerely yours,

Roland L. Taylor

Nelson at the Piano

The Serious Nelson

NELSON EDDY •

New

Movie

Star!

CONCERTS
OPERA
RADIO
TALKIES

A RARE and winning personality, in addition to his glowing qualities as a singer, has advanced this famous young baritone from the concert and opera stage to the even more widely popular field of screen - - - since he was engaged under a long term contract several months ago by Metro-Goldwyn-Mayer. Both musicals and straight films will "mark" the Eddy film career.

Mounting successes each season have embraced a number of radio appearances ranging from individual engagements to *two* different sponsored series, each extending over a period of several weeks—in a steadily expanding career!

CONCERT MANAGEMENT ARTHUR JUDSON, INC., 113 W. 57 St., N. Y. C. (Tel. Cir. 7-6900)
Division Columbia Concerts Corp. of Columbia Broadcasting System, Inc.

LIONEL BARRYMORE

January fifth.

W.D. Eddy, Esq.,
58 Myrtle Street,
Pawtucket, R.I.

My dear Mr. Eddy:-

It was very kind of you to send me a card at Christmas and I thank you most sincerely. It was also very nice of you to suggest that I take care of your son— I should be very glad of the privilege, I assure you, but between us, I think he is very able to take care of himself, and incidentally, of me too.

With all good wishes for your happiness in the New Year, I am,

Sincerely yours,

Lionel Barrymore

LB/W

Beverly Hills, California.

1933

"Naughty Marietta"

Grampa Eddy, Gramma Eddy, Ted Paxon and Nelson
1936 - photo taken by The Providence Journal

Bill, Gramma Eddy, Virginia, Grampa Eddy, Marguerite and Nelson
1936, Pawtucket, Rhode Island

1939

THE PROVIDENCE JOURNAL, FRIDAY, FEBRUARY 17,

All Saints' Church Choir Awards Hagan Medal to Nelson Eddy

Rev. John B. Lyte and William D. Eddy

150 Members and Guests Stand in Honor of Famous Singer's Achievements as Father Receives Award for Son Now on Tour

A TREAT FOR GRANDMA

Mrs Isaac Nelson Eddy got a royal reception yesterday when she went to Loew's State Theatre to hear her famous grandson sing in "Maytime." At the left is Mrs. Eddy's son, William D. Eddy, of Jamestown.

5th October, 1936

Dear Howard:

Something's got to be done about "Merlin Pierce".

Her name is Linn Lambert, address 1817 North Ivar, Hollywood.

She was my secretary for a short time. I discharged her for inefficiency and blab-mouth more than a year ago.

She is now writing articles for fan magazines regarding my home life, love life, experiences with girls, and even the love life of my mother, which is heart rending and embarrassing to the extreme.

Her articles to date are "Hero at Home", October Picture Play; "Worm's Eye-View of Nelson Eddy", November Screen Book; and "Mrs. Eddy's Boy Nelson", November Screenland.

These articles are illustrated by the latest and best MGM photos, eight of them in the last named article.

What is the use of giving careful interviews to bona fide fan writers, and having them personally okeyed, if a wench like this is allowed to have a free hand - apparently with your Still Department's full cooperation?

A bad trick she has is bringing the dope up to date and the impression is that she is now my secretary, relating present day experiences, and presumably with my full consent.

There is something seriously amiss here and I wish you would take steps about it.

Best wishes

Always sincerely

Mr. Howard Strickling
Metro-Goldwyn-Mayer Studios
Culver City, California

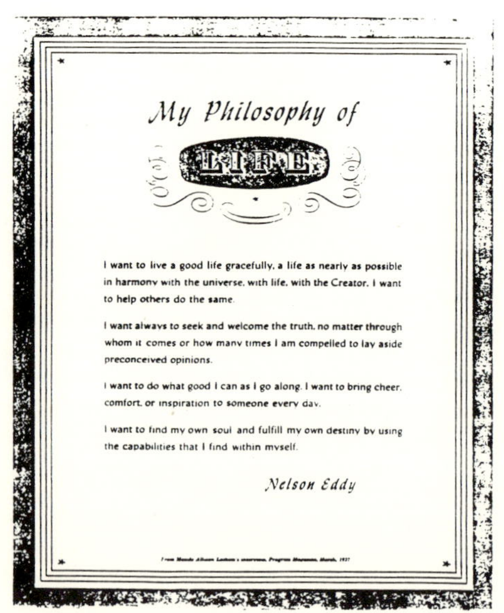

My Philosophy of LIFE

I want to live a good life gracefully, a life as nearly as possible in harmony with the universe, with life, with the Creator. I want to help others do the same.

I want always to seek and welcome the truth, no matter through whom it comes or how many times I am compelled to lay aside preconceived opinions.

I want to do what good I can as I go along. I want to bring cheer, comfort, or inspiration to someone every day.

I want to find my own soul and fulfill my own destiny by using the capabilities that I find within myself.

Nelson Eddy

There are many such stories about Nelson's benevolence and kind-heartedness. He never made idle gestures of help. He never offered his word or a promise without keeping it. He was accessible, the kind of person you could walk up to at a dinner party and ask a favor. If he could help, he would. Many young singers were rescued from grievous errors and their careers improved because of Nelson's generosity and concern.

It wasn't in Nelson's nature not to be honest. He possessed an easy knack of self-analysis and he was generally unashamed by what he found. If anybody sat down and talked to Nelson, he or she would find a very unaffected man, both happy and unhappy at the same time.

Nelson's voice was such a potent instrument in stirring human emotions that millions of women began to let their imaginations run away with them, painting vivid pictures of what romance with Nelson would be like. After "Naughty Marietta", the fans became crazed and unruly which forced Nelson to become more reticent and cautious. The less frenzied fans, those who admired him for his talent, could easily differentiate between reality and fantasy, but the fanatics could not. Thus, a campaign was begun by the more affected fans to win the handsome blond giant for themselves. It wasn't only discerning Hollywood starlets who vied for him, but women of substance and power also set their sights on him. It became a national chase with Nelson dodging the hurdles. Many women followed him from city to city; some never married or formed real relationships in their lives because they were so smitten. For them, imaginary intimacy was enough.

Perhaps too, it was a more innocent era. Their obsessions never turned to the fatal violence many stars are experiencing today. People were more respectful of their idol's and the stars' private lives were not as easily intruded upon.

Although Nelson's image projected a sweetness and vulnerability and his frankness invited friendship, he was very careful never to perpetuate an over involvement with his public. He was always astute and alert to any impending trouble. But he was no match for their unrequited ardor. They converged on him by the thousands. They grabbed at his clothes and pulled at his hair until he became paranoid and frightened. He was forced to guard his privacy all the more fiercely.

MGM on the other hand was excited and delighted by this rousing public response; they wanted Nelson to shoot another picture right away so it could ride the crest of his popularity. Louis B. Mayer hurriedly readied Rudolph Friml's "Rose Marie" for casting. Thanks to fate, the public would once again have their "team". After only one film, Jeanette and Nelson had already become a "team" in the hearts and minds of their public. Now MGM had the opportunity to reinforce this image.

The story line of "Rose Marie" tells about an opera singer who treks into the wilderness in search of her errant brother. The brother is played by Jimmy Stewart; this was his second movie. In 1936 movies were filmed on the studio lot, but "one take" Van Dyke wanted authentic camera shots of real wilderness. He took the entire cast, camera and crew on location to Cascade Lake and Emerald Bay in Lake Tahoe. This was a risky move on Van Dyke's part and no easy task.

In one scene, Nelson was supposed to leap onto his horse and ride off into the wilderness. Still a neophyte, he was eager and overzealous in his attempts to please. Having completely overshot the horse, which galloped off without him, Nelson's flying leap landed him in a clump of sticker bushes. Good naturedly, he tried again, while making self-mocking wise cracks about his ineptitude. It was these humorous occurrences that endeared Nelson to all who worked with him. He knew he had a lot to learn and was deeply grateful to Jeanette and Woody Van Dyke for their help and guidance. Jeanette was always willing to spend time with him. She taught him how to move naturally in front of the camera and how to protect his eyes from the lights. Her wealth of knowledge often staggered him. She made it all look so easy.

Nelson put forth the same effort and determination he always did when challenged. He was a very serious student. For instance, he spent days training himself to become an expert horseman for "Rose Marie". Jeanette always teased Nelson about his thoroughness and his "unsophisticated eagerness". She told a reporter in 1936, "Nelson is the least theatrical artist I've ever known." There was a great deal of respect between them. Woody Van Dyke referred to Nelson as "Kid", and to Jeanette as "Honey". Nelson had a flare for old-world gallantry and Jeanette loved his manners and unassuming politeness.

Usually, they were on the set for twelve hours. If they weren't too tired, Jeanette and Nelson would gather the cast for impromptu entertainment by singing to the local residents. There was always a lot of good natured ribbing between cast and crew with Nelson and Jeanette right in the middle.

By now, Nelson was becoming accustomed to playing the stalwart hero usually squeezed into some rigid uniform riding atop a beautiful stallion. He came across as the trustworthy friend while Jeanette matched his vulnerability with a kittenish playfulness. It takes considerable acting ability to emote lyrics from your heart while stuffed into a ridiculously tight uniform that held your body rigid. In retrospect, it's a tribute to Nelson and his style of performing that he managed to get away with it at all.

Who could ever forget hearing *Indian Love Call* or remembering the *Totem Tom Tom* scene with hundreds of indians in full war paint and a full orchestra playing in the background. These were light operettas and it was expected that when Nelson gathered the mounties for serious discussion, he would burst into song.

Of the eight movies the "team" made together, "Rose Marie" is the most remembered. "Variety" praised the movie calling it a "box office honey". The mountie hat wasn't very flattering to Nelson's handsome good looks, but he was a stickler for authenticity. In 1970 when the Canadian Mounted Police retired their "mountie uniform", a picture of Nelson as Sergeant Bruce in full dress accompanied the story. The scene of Nelson and Jeanette singing *Indian Love Call* was to become a classic as well. Throughout the years, this scene has been parodied in a variety of skits using both satire and comedy. It gave Nelson and Jeanette a place in our cultural heritage. MGM paid Nelson exactly $1,000 a week for making "Rose Marie". He could have made $300,000 a year on a straight concert tour.

In November of 1936, Nelson and Jeanette made their first commercial recording together for RCA Victor Records. *Indian Love Call* was on one side and *Ah, Sweet Mystery of Life* on the other. An instant best seller, the record remained in the top 100 recordings for years. Twenty-five years later, when Nelson received a gold record for selling over one million copies, he declared, "That sure was a mighty slow Indian."

Robert Armbruster met Nelson when he began recording for RCA Victor Records in 1936. He became fast friends with Nelson, as well as Jeanette, and many other stars who signed with RCA. Nicknamed Bobby by those who knew him well, he reminisced about "those wonderful times" with me. Bobby tells of a typical recording session with Nelson, while sternly reminding me that those recording sessions were nerve wracking for most singers:

> But not for Nelson. He could cut twenty-two sides or eleven records at one time then go off to a concert or work on a movie. The sessions were usually three hours long. You were lucky to get one song done in an hour, because in those days it took quite a while to get set up to do a record. They were electrical records. A waxed disc was used to record the song. While the recording was being made, there wasn't any ability to manipulate, amplify or change a voice as there is today. Therefore, if you made an error, there was no way to correct the slightest mistake. You had to start over with a new disc.

Bobby was always astounded that Nelson could make a record on the first try. Nelson was always on key, with extraordinary timing and perfect diction.

Radio was a unique medium. It demanded that one learn a new script each week. Live and on the air, it was never boring and often times bordered on the ridiculous. Radio stars had to be able to camouflage mistakes and shoot from the hip. Nelson was a regular on the Chase and Sanborn Hour. Bobby Armbruster was the musical director of the show. It was one of the most popular radio shows on the air. Hosted by Don Ameche, it starred Nelson, Edgar Bergen and Charlie McCarthy with Dorothy Lamour and W.C. Fields. On the show, Nelson had a chance to let loose with his comedic style of bantering. The audience always wanted more. Bobby laughed remembering how they put the show together:

> Rehearsals were often held over the entire weekend. I usually rehearsed all three days while Nelson varied his rehearsals based on the condition of his voice. Dorothy Lamour and Don Ameche usually showed up at Saturday rehearsals and Nelson would join them for script changes. The orchestra would always rehearse again right before the show. Charlie McCarthy and W.C. Fields were just as funny in rehearsals as they were on the air and they usually had everybody in stitches. The atmosphere on the show was warm and friendly, no one was cut throat.

Bobby pointed out that Nelson's influence was very strong. He never tolerated back biting or unfairness.

Shortnin' Bread became Nelson's trademark on the show. Bobby remembers:

> He withstood merciless teasing about this rendition from Charlie McCarthy and it associated him with the song for the rest of his life. He kept the song as a staple in both his concertizing and radio shows inyears to come.
>
> Nelson was one of the most well-rounded musicians I have ever met. He was the ultimate musician. He knew how every instrument worked---the intrinsic combination of rhythm and timing. He saw music in terms of the whole; the voice in perfect cohesion with the accompanist. He strived for perfection.

If it is true that like attracts like, then Nelson and Art Rush represent the prime example. Art Rush possessed the same respect for family and love of traditional values as Nelson did. He was Nelson's manager for twenty-two years.

Art came to Hollywood to audition for a show at RCA Victor Records. While auditioning, he noticed that RCA was in the process of destroying the costly Vitaphone recording presses previously used to provide sound for motion pictures. He created and tested the utilization of these old 16 inch records to prerecord the 30 minute radio shows. It was a great success and Art became the pioneer of the electrical transcription business. His success as the creator of transcribed radio led him to be named the West Coast Manager of RCA Victor in 1932 at the young age of 25. Art and Nelson met at RCA where Art recorded Nelson, Jeanette MacDonald, Kathryn Grayson, Glenn Miller, Lilly Pons, and Benny Goodman.

Five years later, Art became Managing Director of Columbia Management of California. While at Columbia, he managed Nelson along with Jackie Gleason, Mary Martin, Orson Wells and Eugene Ormandy. After three years, he resigned from Columbia Management to start his own company. In 1939, Art Rush, Inc. had its first client, Nelson Eddy. Art later discovered Mario Lanza and managed him during his career. In recent years he managed Roy Rogers and Dale Evans and their museum "Apple Valley".

Art Rush became Nelson's closest friend. Nelson was responsible for introducing Art to his wife, Mary Jo Matthews, a young starlet at MGM whose publicity picture Art had seen in the paper. He called Nelson and asked him to arrange a meeting and Nelson happily complied. Art and Mary Jo had two sons, William and Robert. Robert Nelson Rush, is named after Robert Armbruster and Nelson Eddy. Art and Mary Jo were the closest of friends with Nelson and Ann Eddy. They shared many memorable times together.

Bobby Armbruster related a wonderful story about Art Rush and their radio days together. After the show, Art, a couple of arrangers, Edouard Lippe, Ted Paxson and Bobby used to go over to Nelson's house for something to eat. Nelson was living on Maple Avenue in Beverly Hills then, and he had a great Spanish cook who loved people. She would put out an array of the best Mexican food around. As Bobby tells it:

> We'd all go over to eat after the show. Now, Nelson and Art loved magic tricks. Well, Art was one of the sweetest guys in the world, and he would always have some kind of magic or slight of hand trick to show Nelson. He'd be so excited about fooling him. Since Nelson always left right after the show, the rest of us would stick around a few minutes to make sure everything was cleaned up before heading over to his house.
>
> Art would say, "Hey, Bobby, wait till you see this trick. Nelson will never be able to do it." Then Art would show me exactly how the trick was done and I'd say, "Yeah, this one will get him. See you over at Nelson's." As soon as Art was out of that building, I'd rush over to the phone and call Nelson. I'd describe the entire trick to him explaining exactly how it worked. By the time I got over to Nelson's, Art was ready to do the trick. We'd all gather round and watch Nelson with this deadpan expression say, "Gee, that looks hard, Art, but let me try it." Well, of course, he would duplicate the trick perfectly, keeping this straight face the whole time. Poor Art, he was stymied. He used to say "That guy Nelson is a genius. I can't find a trick he can't do." This went on for weeks before Art finally discovered our ruse.
>
> Art always went to a novelty shop on Vine Street to find the most difficult magic tricks he could. The store owner was beside himself so we finally had to tell Art the truth. For years afterwards, Art still tried to one-up Nelson with new tricks. As it turned out,

> Nelson never was fooled. He always caught on to them.

Bobby believes it was Nelson's "yankee curiosity". He always had to get to the bottom of everything.

Don Ameche, Edgar Bergen, Bobby Armbruster, Art, Ted, Lippe---they were a close knit group of professional, yet personal friends. Don Ameche described Nelson during those years:

> His most impressive characteristic is his terrific will-power. He really likes to have fun, and at a formal party once, he did an actual burlesque strip tease in tails. He is a wonderful host, but he is extremely ethical. He would never do anything that might hurt anyone. He is a technical student of music. He's always a gentlemen and holds his liquor like a man.

When Art Rush was interviewed in 1976, he was asked to define his philosophy and explain which star of all he worked with he admired the most. Art explained that he always restricted himself to work with people he liked:

> I turned down some very fine talent because I didn't believe in their conduct of life, or the fact that I couldn't, in all honesty, go out and sell them. In all my associations with the greatest stars, Nelson Eddy was one of the finest men I have ever met. He was brilliant. He was the most honest, finest individual that you could ever meet. He could have been a president of a corporation just as easily as he could be a performer at MGM or sing in his concerts. He was number one in my book.

Mary Jo Rush passed away September 30, 1988. Art, injured in an accident, died January 1, 1989 at the age of

81. Their sons, Bob and Bill, shared with me many happy childhood memories of visits to the Eddy home and cherish the generous gifts Nelson and Ann gave them. Bob Rush has Nelson's sterling hairbrush set. A beautifully carved sideboard from the Eddy's occupies a prominent place in Bill Rush's home today.

Chapter Eight

The last thing on Nelson's mind one fateful Sunday in April was falling in love. He was feeling rested after his last concert tour and was looking forward to visiting with friends. He was often invited to Doris Kenyon's house to play tennis and share conversation. Ann Denitz Franklin was also invited to Doris's that day. Nelson and Ann had met several years before and liked each other then. They talked quietly as afternoon turned into evening. Ann even accompanied Nelson on the piano as he entertained the guests. Nelson knew he had met a woman who was a "good audience", not in any way a prima donna. He later described his feeling about that fateful evening, "I found myself talking to a very intelligent and attractive woman. I felt that here was a woman I should like to know and keep for a friend."

They met again at Doris's house. He became her escort to parties. Nelson described the relationship's beginnings as "a slow, sound thing"; they felt comfortable with each other. Nelson saw in Ann a woman he could trust and this was of the utmost importance to him.

Since his name was always linked with a famous star, the public visualized Nelson with a glamourous woman. This was the perfect camouflage for Nelson and Ann as they quietly fell in love. They attended parties and previews, they often went dancing, but were very careful never to show any public demonstrations of their love. They purposely never touched in public or made announced entrances. They avoided press agents and reporters whenever they could. Because no one expected Nelson to be involved with an unknown, Hollywood dismissed for the most part their togetherness as inconsequential. Only Isabel and Nelson's close knit group of friends recognized the blossoming of true love.

Doris Kenyon was well aware of the love developing between her good friends. Later she described Ann to a reporter friend. "Ann's casualness about everything, all that she accomplishes so quickly and graciously is certainly admirable. She is always deflecting attention from herself and pointing to the worthwhile qualities in other people. I think her strength lies in her capacity to live through others, because this is how she expresses herself best." Doris knew that Nelson and Ann were wonderfully suited for each other. Ann was known in Hollywood circles. She had the same personality and bearing when she was married to the artistic director, Sidney Franklin. This ability to divert attention from herself was a very clever and practical characteristic.

Ann had established herself as a superior hostess. One of those rare people who could invite many people to her home and provide the perfect meal, beautifully presented with elegant table setting and style, yet be as unobtrusive as possible, allowing her guests to enjoy themselves without her interfering in any way.

Ann understood marriage and its pitfalls. She had been married fifteen years and was the mother of a young son, Sidney Franklin, Jr., who Nelson adored.

Although Ann was not a trained musician, she had a wonderful ear for music. She could always tell when Nelson was off-key. She was his favorite audience and his best critic. Possessing a delightful sense of humor, she was downright funny just as Nelson was. Her humor was gut level, her laugh so hearty and contagious that she'd often have to leave the room to gain control of herself again.

Ann was one of three children born to Philip and Julia Denitz. Her father, a Russian immigrant, settled the family in Trinidad, Colorado where Ann, her sister Irene and brother Herbert were born. They later moved to Amarillo, Texas where Ann grew up. The family used to spend their summers in California. It was during this time that Philip met Abbott Keeney, a land developer. The town's historical documents show that Philip Denitz and Abbott Keeney were instrumental in starting the town of Venice, California. Philip Denitz became a retail merchant and the family finally made Venice their permanent residence. Ann and Irene attended the Girl's Collegiate School in Los Angeles. She married Sidney Franklin in 1918 and their only child, Sidney Jr. was born six years later.

As a producer's wife, Ann knew the many angles and problems of the movie world. During fifteen years of marriage to Sidney, she developed a keen understanding of the problems inherent in this world of make believe. She successfully steered her marriage through troubled waters, but eventually the marriage faltered. Louella Parsons didn't help much when she printed an article hinting that Sidney was infatuated with Conrad Nagel's wife. The Nagels and the Franklins had beach houses next door to each other and were friends as well as neighbors. It was doubly difficult for Ann to have her pain become public knowledge. Ann and Sidney divorced in 1933 and Sidney married Ruth Nagel shortly thereafter.

The studio, continuing to give Nelson co-star billing, added publicity to match his new status. Praise was forthcoming from the critics, but Nelson knew that he had to live up to this "success" or quickly become a has-been. He suffered anxiety attacks and questioned his sanity for staying in Hollywood. No one will ever know the trauma and inner turmoil he suffered because of the demands of his overnight success. It took great strength and fortitude to hold on to the simple, yet righteous, code of ethics by which he lived.

It was bad enough that he couldn't live or breathe without millions of women swooning. Potent and more harmful rumors began to spread as the fans transferred their screen romancing into the illusion that Nelson and Jeanette were real-life lovers. These rumors spread quickly after the public viewed "Naughty Marietta". "Look at how they stare into each others eyes, see how he touched her", they sighed.

The chemistry of a "team" is often undefinable. There have been other teams who romanced each other on the screen. William Powell and Myrna Loy made thirteen films together. Fred Astaire and Ginger Rogers, and Olivia De Havilland and Errol Flynn---all of these pairs made more films together than Nelson and Jeanette, yet none of them captured the hearts of their fans with such demanding force. The undefinable MacDonald-Eddy chemistry lasted a lifetime. Even now, twenty-five years after Nelson's death, the romantic linking of Nelson and Jeanette still lives in the minds of many.

The rumors about "the team" took varying courses. Some said Jeanette and Nelson were jealous of each other and didn't get along at all. Other rumors wove intricate tales of their love for each other. Jeanette MacDonald and Nelson Eddy were becoming a legend. Neither of them expected such status, nor did they flaunt it---they were simply astonished! Watch any one of their movies today and you will see that, together, they emote a beautiful harmonious cinematic performance that should have been enough for anybody, but it wasn't! It was inevitable that the public who laughed and cried with them as they spun magical tales and grand illusions would conclude they were lovers, even married in real life. It was a misconception they were never able to correct---a misconception which would bring pain and sorrow to their families in later years.

In Hollywood, Nelson was already the consternation of all the press agents, but Jeanette wasn't all that publicity conscious either. If they had been headline minded at all, they might have done something to deflect the suspicion that they were sweethearts. That idea never occurred to Nelson and Jeanette; they were busy with their own lives. Jeanette had her friends and Nelson had his. Outside the studio, there was little socializing between them. They had different needs and dispositions and chose their life styles accordingly. The more untruths that were written, the more guarded Nelson became.

In his three years of movie making, Jeanette was the only female star Nelson had ever worked with. He liked her sincerity and idealism. She was always honest and up front in her relationships. Above all, Nelson respected Jeanette's sense of values. Her standards were as high and consistent as his own. They both were respected, not because they demanded it, but rather because they deserved it. They got along well most of the time, but admitted to their own idiosyncrasies and eccentricities. In fact, they more than got along, they were friends.

Every star of the 1930's and 1940's had fan clubs. Nelson's and Jeanette's were the most popular. Fans couldn't sign up fast enough. These clubs were a popular means of sharing information, and the stars, for the most part, respected and honored the clubs. Through the clubs, over zealous fans could get autographs, pictures and intimate knowledge about their idols. Fan clubs even gave out the addresses of the stars proving that this was a far more gracious and trusting era. "The Nelson Eddy Music Club" was formed in 1935. The first club magazine was called "The Nelson Eddy Fan Club News", later changed to "The Shooting Star". The Jeanette MacDonald International Fan Club publication is "The Golden Comet" and has been in existence since 1938.

While on concert tour, Nelson couldn't even walk through the corridor of his hotel or appear in a public dining room without being molested. He was forced to hire body guards to protect him from the frantic fans. He could no longer go to the theater or walk into the backstage entrance of the concert halls where he was appearing without being besieged by his adoring public. He had to be taken into the buildings by an underground route or by guards. He hid in locked washrooms while guards cleared a path for him. He could have easily retreated, but his intrinsic belief in fairness wouldn't let him. In truth, Nelson did not feel fame was worth these penalties, yet he tried to remain humorous and upstanding, a thoroughly American young man. But he was becoming more fearful and even cynical about appearing among his own people. For those who knew Nelson and his deep rooted distaste for any kind of extravagant hero worship, the impact on him was apparent. Nelson retreated and spent several days visiting with Bill and Marguerite. Bill Eddy often told Ginny of his concerns over Nelson's fears.

During his concert tour, Ann seemed very far away. Nelson, enduring the hardships of the road better than most, was busy catching trains, fighting off a bad cold, driving through blizzards, besieged as always by his lovesick fans. But in his mind and heart, he kept remembering Ann and their quiet evenings of shared togetherness.

Nelson was not happy with MGM's hold on him. He was upset and disappointed that MGM wouldn't lend him to Universal for the role opposite Irene Dunne in "Showboat". His only escape used to be his concert tours, but because of

Ann, he just exchanged one form of grief for another. He missed Ann. There was no solution to his discontent.

He was love sick, home sick, weary and depressed. He wrote to a friend, "I'm sitting here in my hotel room not having much fun. I had dinner sent up and ate alone. The fans are outside the door. If there were just one or two, I could give them an autograph and they'd go, but there are hundreds. Every two hours, the management makes them go away, but they come right back." He finally called Ann and told her that he couldn't bear another long separation.

As the most eligible bachelor in America, he was at the public's mercy. Women could have ideas about him and he had no protection. He often felt frightened and helpless. The lonely junkets left him vulnerable to the many strangers who constantly surrounded him. He had to avoid nightclubs and public places. He was constantly harassed which only made him more depressed and self-conscious. In self defense, he had little choice but to withdraw into a shell. His fans didn't see it, but his critics certainly did and they were quick to criticize him for it. They called him reticent, wooden and stand-offish. He even told a reporter that he felt he could never relax, lest he would say or do something his fans would dislike. But when he met Ann and fell in love, he realized that while he was trying so hard to keep his fans happy, he had forgotten to find happiness for himself.

Nelson needed his solitude. He needed to keep ruthless intrusions out of his private life. One night, he returned home to find a group of strangers standing in his living room and he broke down completely. How they managed to gain entry is unimportant, but the effect on him was traumatic. This episode had a lasting effect on him. He became edgy and nervous for long periods at a time and for the rest of his life - he would hesitate before entering his home.

When he finally had the opportunity to put everything into perspective, he realized that he was performing a service, rather a heroic service if you will. To millions upon millions of wishful women who snatched their hours from daily cares in those movie houses, Nelson was their prince charming. If you watch those movies today, it is possible to imagine, even feel, how Nelson stole their hearts away.

He surmised that Hollywood was divided into five parts, working cinema people, the has-beens, the silent picture stars, local society and ex-wives along with the general public. It's the local society that starts the rumors about actors, while motion picture people are hard at work with little time for any of the froth. Nelson, totally frustrated, let loose with his real feelings about Hollywood in an article in the "Los Angeles Times". "Movie actors and actresses are forced to lead an unnatural life. When they come to Hollywood their personalities are changed. They must be selfish and ruthless or they won't get beyond their first feature role. In all my life, I have never seen such a bunch of conceited people as there are here with the possible exception of those working in opera," exclaimed Nelson. He complained of having to change his phone number each week, and he avoided the Hollywood party circuit. The parties all followed the same pattern. "Like a game, you get eight or more people together, invite photographers to crash the gates and take pictures of everyone in every conceivable place and pose." To Nelson who hated pretense, this was not a party, but a publicity stunt.

Nelson preferred the exceptions. Jeanette MacDonald was an exception, as was Basil Rathbone. They gave parties because they wanted to see their friends, not because they had a mad desire to see their names and pictures in print. Nelson, too, was the exception!

Whether Nelson would admit it or not, he was a conservative. With his New England heritage and courtly bearing, he spoke with perfect enunciation which gave him an almost old-world air. He was reserved, a good son to his mother and father, very meticulous about his manners and his method of doing things. He hung on tight to his standards, to his ideals. It was no easy feat. One can accuse him of being old-fashioned and not modern, but I believe he was probably modern in his desires, but certainly old-fashioned in his beliefs. This gave him an added air of mystery that made women want him all the more.

His radio shows, the movies, his concerts, his studies...he managed them perfectly as if he were head of a large corporation. He was a frequent guest on "Vick's Open House" and "Ford Sunday Evening Hour" radio programs. Nelson had finally made it to the top, and he did it without changing his personality or his habits. Nelson, the enigma, remained as unaffected as ever.

Isabel and Nelson moved into a bigger home where all the relatives could stay when they visited. Isabel had a wonderful time buying furniture and hiring a staff. They had Hans, a jack-of-all-trades, to help around the house, a cook and a maid to help Isabel. Nelson also hired a private secretary to help handle business matters. Up to now his life had been dedicated to singing. A perfectionist, he never gave anything less than his best. His practice, studies, and art work commanded all his time and effort. His career now embraced all facets of entertainment, the motion pictures, radio and concerts stage plus hundreds of guest appearances.

When Jeanette met and fell in love with Gene Raymond, Nelson was overjoyed about the romance. Both were his friends, and although he didn't introduce them, he knew instinctively their personalities meshed. It was an answer to his prayers---now millions of fans would be able to see that there was nothing between Jeanette and himself.

After Jeanette announced her engagement to Gene Raymond, Nelson immediately sat down and wrote a delightful article called "Gene Raymond is a Lucky Guy". He related in detail all the wonderful qualities Jeanette possessed. Gene and Nelson knew each other long before Jeanette came into the picture. Jeanette loved to interject that Nelson and Gene had gone on several camping trips together, and she knew the habits of both. Nelson would often joke to Gene, "You may be her main man, but I'm her leading man."

Jeanette and Nelson often discussed their perspective mates. Jeanette was the first to notice how much more relaxed Nelson was since he had begun to see Ann. She was pleased he had finally found someone he could share his life with. Isabel was also thrilled at the new found happiness in her son's life.

Ann was Nelson's saving grace in a town which was not congenial to his philosophy of living. She could see Nelson's unrest and reticence around strangers. She knew how hard it was for him to adjust to the ways of Hollywood. She knew that trust was the key to Nelson's heart. There never was anyone else for Nelson except Ann, but they wisely chose to wait a few years before marrying. Actually, it was Ann who made the decision to wait. A very clever woman, she recognized how important it was for Nelson to establish himself in his career. She had her work cut out for her. There were many issues to consider. She could hardly help but be jealous. Everywhere she turned, there were thousands of adoring women wanting Nelson, loving him, touching him. Although she trusted him with all of her heart, Nelson's concerts constantly took him away for long periods. Ann needed time to accept what her life would be like if she married Nelson. And Nelson wasn't always perfect either. One night during a party at the Trocadero, Nelson had his hand on Ann's knee while batting his eyes at another woman when Ann spotted the flirting. She got up and walked out on him and left Nelson sitting there. Ann took a taxi home and Nelson followed in hot pursuit. There were no more such instances.

She carefully nurtured her relationship with him---her devotion was admirable. She was always there for him as he was for her. Sidney remembers his mother telling him, "Everybody wants him, but I have him." The hardships ahead were barely considered against the many joys which they brought to each other.

Ann and Nelson possessed a spirit of camaraderie, a friendship shared and a radiant togetherness. Ann combined sweetness and a mature womanhood. She was never a public figure, nor did she wish to become one. "One ego is enough," Nelson would say. Nelson didn't care whether she worked or not, nor whether they were rich or poor. "I'm really not so temperamental. I prepare carefully for everything I do. My business is singing," he said. "Ann loves me enough to understand fame and its game. She's knowledgeable in her own worth to be a backdrop, so to speak, if she has to. So the New Englander in me turned out to be stronger than the Hollywood in me."

In 1937 when MGM readied another operetta for filming, there was no question as to who should co-star with whom. Nelson and Jeanette were teamed for "Maytime". MGM had finally learned what the fans already knew. Only "the team" would do! Everyone was happy about the decision except Mayer. Hope ran high on the set as preparations were made to start filming.

Irving Thalberg, the young movie wizard, was supervising the production. Even though he and Mayer didn't get along of late---Thalberg was a fighter. He managed to ward off Mayer's constant barbs long enough to accomplish some brilliant shots. Although Mayer's private life was usually torrid and scandalous, he took a very puritanical view of life when it came to his pictures. He wanted everything on screen to be squeaky clean and all American. The story of "Maytime" was about a single man and a married woman attracted to each other. Mayer was not at all happy with this scenario, so he constantly heckled Thalberg. Thalberg held firm in his own style of interpretation until one autumn day when it all came to a halt. On September 14th, while right in the middle of filming, Thalberg had a heart attack and died at the age of 37. The entire production was thrown into turmoil. Mayer immediately closed down the production, personally taking over the film. The original scenes of "Maytime" are in storage in the MGM Classics' Division archives and have never been viewed by the public.

The story and script were revised and rewritten. Major changes were made, certain characters were eliminated, footage that had already been shot was scrapped and a new approach was outlined by Mayer. The film, originally shot in technicolor, was returned to black and white because Louis B. claimed that technicolor hurt his eyes. Hunt Stromberg took over as producer.

A further complication was Nelson's schedule. He had been booked for a forty-three day concert tour and was unable to postpone it. Therefore, all of his scenes were shot at one time making a shambles of the film crew's schedule. After many trials and tribulations, the film was finally finished.

Today, "Maytime" is perceived as the most critically acclaimed of the films Nelson and Jeanette made. It was a tremendous box office success and succeeded in keeping Nelson and Jeanette flying high. Everyone loved "the team". Jeanette, deeply in love with Gene Raymond at the time, added dramatic emotionalism and flair to her acting. Of all the pictures Jeanette made, "Maytime" was her personal favorite. In "Maytime" both Nelson and Jeanette were afforded the opportunity to do serious acting.

"Maytime" is said to have the most beautiful springtime scene ever created in film history. The "New York Times" called it "a picture to treasure" and "Time Magazine" deemed "Maytime" the best entertainment of 1937. It is listed in the Encyclopedia Britannica as the most outstanding picture of 1937.

Herman Bing, a regular in the Nelson and Jeanette operettas, was delightful as ever. Nelson dearly loved Herman. He would laugh long and loud as Herman rolled his rrr's while playing the part of Nelson's frustrated music teacher. To Nelson, Herman Bing was the funniest fellow he ever worked with. Nelson would choke in the middle of a song, miss one of his lines or kill a couple of takes just because Herman made him laugh so hard he couldn't stop. Herman made four films with Nelson and managed to break up the cast with laughter every time. He was a kind and loved man. After World War II, when the frothy operettas had become passe, Herman went from studio to studio looking for work, but his kind of comedy was no longer in demand. At the time he committed suicide in 1947, he had been out of work for two years.

In January 1937, Jeanette was voted Best Female Singer by the "Modern Screen Magazine" poll and Nelson was voted the Best Male Singer. By now the fan clubs were growing to enormous proportions. After the release of

"Maytime", Nelson's fan club wrote irate letters to the movie magazines and to the studio complaining that he was given much less screen time than Jeanette. This was to become a consistently repeated complaint by both fan clubs---the fans were that strong. MGM, reeling from their latest success, reasoned why not separate the two stars and make the public pay twice for them. MGM promptly scheduled Nelson to make "Rosalie" with Eleanor Powell.

The timing of Mayer's proclamation was well planned to coincide with the latest rumors since Eleanor Powell was romantically linked with Nelson at the time. A simple hello kiss greeted Nelson as he returned to the studio after his three month concert tour; unfortunately for Eleanor, she didn't check to see if the reporters were lurking as she reached for him. The next day the newspapers extolled their great "love affair". It was an embarrassing situation for both of them.

Ann sat by quietly, unselfishly watching Nelson as he gained stature. Carefully choosing his battles, he tried to quickly dispel each rumor. Ann was always close by but usually in the background. She attended every rehearsal and every radio broadcast of Nelson's. Fifty-one Sundays in a row, she sat in the front row of the NBC auditorium. After the show, Don Ameche, Edgar Bergen, Bobby Armbruster and the rest of the gang would join Nelson and Ann for a buffet supper at someone's home.

When Dad Eddy retired in 1937, he and Marguerite moved into the old Eddy house on Myrtle Street in Pawtucket so Ginny could have the additional cultural advantages. The house in Jamestown became a summer home.

Nelson celebrated his dad's retirement by inviting him to California for a visit. He knew his father was dying to meet Mae West and he wanted to give his Dad something he'd never forget. Ginny laughingly recalls the story:

> Dad's pin-up girl at that time was Mae West and his ambition was to see her in person. He had no more stepped off the train, when he went to the Chase and Sanborn Radio Show rehearsal with Nelson. They were doing a show which had Mae West in the cast. It was the "Adam and Eve" skit which was considered quite shocking at the time. Anyway, Dad had his picture taken with Edgar Bergen, Charlie McCarthy, Nelson and Mae West. Nelson was grinning and Dad was looking at Mae in all the right places. She autographed her picture to him "come up and see me sometime." It was a great success!

Isabel and Ann were very much alike. They both understood the demands of fame. They both were willing to uphold the privacy and trust which Nelson held so dear. Ann was even getting accustomed to the constant police protection surrounding Nelson. She was fast becoming a strong influence in his life and career just as Isabel had been. In fact, Isabel and Ann agreed on most issues involving his happiness. He was the last of a vanishing breed, a true Renaissance Man, and most women knew it. Ann, above all, knew how fortunate she was to have Nelson's love and trust, and she was intent on protecting him.

While Nelson was paired with Eleanor to film "Rosalie", Jeanette was scheduled to make "The Firefly" with Allan Jones. Jeanette's wedding was only a few months away and she was very preoccupied with the final plans. While "the team" was separated to fulfill their contract obligations, the fans were checking out the latest rumors as to why "the team" had split up.

Regardless, "Rosalie" proved to be another box office success for MGM. It also marked the screen debut of Ilona Massey. Ilona was a Hungarian beauty and a prize find of MGM studios. There were great Cole Porter tunes and plenty of Eleanor's creative tap dancing routines. Nelson was in uniform once again, this time as a West Point Cadet. Cole Porter even wrote the title song to "Rosalie" at Louis B. Mayer's request. It was an expensive production with lavish sets constructed for the wedding march procession and Eleanor's dance numbers.

MGM asked Nelson and Eleanor to perform scenes from "Rosalie" on their weekly radio show, the Maxwell House Radio Hour. This meant he would have to sing on two rival radio programs. The Chase and Sanborn producers were torn by the thought of their star's beguiling voice singing about coffee drinkers for a competitor. Legally, Nelson was scheduled to endorse the merits of Maxwell House Coffee by participating in the "Rosalie" broadcast. Everyone was quite upset by the situation including the lawyers and advertising firms. As the morning of the first rehearsal rolled around on the Maxwell House Coffee set, tension prevailed. In walked Nelson, smiling brightly, raring to go, wearing a sandwich board which read, "I drink Sanka". "That guy will be the death of me," an NBC employee wheezed with laughter. The tension quickly passed as everybody broke up with laughter. This and other gags staged by the so called "proper" Mr. Eddy were constant.

By now Eleanor and Nelson were good friends. He liked and respected her as a person and he enjoyed making the movie with her. It was a fresh change of pace for both of them. Woody Van Dyke directed and Frank Morgan, another "team" regular, joined them this time around. Ilona

Massey also made a good friend in Nelson and he would continue to help and support her career.

Eleanor Powell wrote the forward for Philip Constanza's book "The Films of Jeanette MacDonald and Nelson Eddy" published in 1976. She stated that there was a feeling of joy and happiness on the set while making "Rosalie" with Nelson. Eleanor described Nelson as a warm and sensitive, humorous and happy individual, just the opposite of the stoic cardboard Canadian Mountie Policeman that his critics often labeled him. Eleanor remembered Nelson played practical jokes on the set. He was very endearing; everyday he would bring one red rose to her dressing room, meant to show an appreciation of her talent. They remained friends for many years after "Rosalie". In later years, when Eleanor visited the grave of her father in Hollywood Memorial Cemetery, she would always lay a rose on the grave of Isabel Eddy. To this day, Nelson's fan club also places a rose on Eleanor's grave, as she was a very special friend to him.

Chapter Nine

The marriage of Jeanette and Gene Raymond was a most successful blend of personalities. All my research steadfastly confirms this fact. All who knew Ann and Nelson as well as Jeanette and Gene have literally been infuriated by certain fan publications and misguided rumors which have tried to dispel the happiness that all four had in their marriages. They were mature when they chose their mates and they both chose well.

But they couldn't win for losing. No matter what they did, the public found fault. The fan clubs by now had grown to staggering memberships. They would fight and argue about trivial matters analyzing every shot of their beloved star. Jeanette and Nelson both tried to deter the illusions the public had of them. But it turned around and back-fired on them. Nelson received thousands of fan letters saying how miserable he must feel about losing Jeanette. He must be in tears, taking his loss very hard. It made Nelson even angrier that the media and the public pictured him with his heart broken to jagged bits, beyond all mending, because he could not have the girl he courted on the screen. What more could he do to convince them. Hadn't he been forthright and honest?

I would like to clarify that through diligent research and factual interviews with those who knew the innermost workings of their lives, there was no love affair between Nelson and Jeanette. On June 16, 1937, Nelson sang *I Love You Truly* and *Oh Perfect Love* at Jeanette's and Gene's wedding. Right after the wedding, he drove straight to Ann's house.

Talk about shattering expectations, movie fans throughout the world suffered a terrible shock when they woke up to find that Jeanette MacDonald had married Gene Raymond. Surely, this cannot be, they cried, the real romance is between Nelson and Jeanette.

Jeanette's comments about the rumors were consistent with Nelson's and, in an interview by Roger Carroll, Jeanette stated:

> Rumors like this either amuse you highly or they make you mad. At first, we both were amused. We both had our sense of humor---then. We have since gotten a dent in that sense of humor because of fantastic stories about our respective private lives. Nelson says that all kinds of distortions have been printed about him. I'm willing to believe him, because I know about myself. I'm beginning to see Nelson's viewpoint---that what we do at home shouldn't concern the public, as long as our pictures satisfy the public. Nelson has been very severely criticized for that viewpoint. But he's a man who sticks by his own beliefs. And I understand him. If a star wants to make a show of himself, let him, say I. But if another star wants to live a quiet life, let him have his quiet life. Also, I can applaud Nelson's unwillingness to talk about love and women. I defy any woman not to respect such a man.

In 1938, the fans were clamoring for "the team", and MGM obliged by bringing Nelson and Jeanette back together again to make "Girl of the Golden West". This would be their fourth film together and the public was thrilled.

Nelson, deeply in love with Ann, was holding his own; while Jeanette, happily married to Gene, was feeling happy and optimistic. The script of "Girl of the Golden West" offered her a chance to play a rough, unsophisticated frontier woman which was a far cry from her past screen images.

Nelson's relationship with Jeanette had discreetly changed in the past few years. Before, Nelson the neophyte, was in awe of Jeanette's knowledge and ability. Now the roles began to reverse a bit. It was Jeanette's turn to be staggered by Nelson's energy and savvy. She marveled at the way Nelson could do a radio program, a motion picture and rehearse for a concert tour all at the same time, especially since he practiced five hours a day when preparing to go on tour. She was impressed by his versatility.

Nelson, who always did his own stunts, had a tough one to master in "Girl of the Golden West". He had to wrap a leather snake whip around Jeanette. He practiced the stunt for only a week before having to shoot it on film. "Standing there, waiting for that whip to curl around me was no picnic," exclaimed Jeanette. Nelson made his usual wise crack, snapped the whip and it was all over. There were no casualties.

Although "Girl of the Golden West" didn't have the same zip as the other movies "the team" had made, just listening to Nelson and Jeanette sing the Sigmund Romberg music was enough to satisfy the fans. They flocked to the theaters to the tune of another box office hit, but not of the same magnitude. Both Nelson and Jeanette wished Louis B. Mayer would give them new material to work with.

Nelson and Jeanette were often stymied by their fans' thinking. After shooting a scene which called for Nelson to treat Jeanette roughly, one reporter wrote of their "battle royal". The article emphasized that the battle was a personal one---a major feud. Nelson took the time to write the reporter a letter chiding him about reporting on a movie scene and not on real life.

Most of the rumors about their "feuds" appeared during the time when the studio co-starred them with other people. After all, it was the studio bosses who teamed them together and it was the studio bosses who separated them. As Nelson aptly put it, "We don't decide what pictures we should do or shouldn't do. We'd be fools to feud, especially when working harmoniously together is bread and butter to both of us."

The public wanted information on Nelson's love life, not just his latest picture. Where is Nelson? Why isn't he making the Hollywood circuit? Because Nelson held the loyalty of all who knew him, it is no surprise that hardly any publicity leaked out regarding his romance with Ann. Nelson kept Ann his well guarded secret longer than any other star possibly could have. Very few articles were printed about his feelings, but then, he trusted very few people. He dodged questions, while holding Ann close to his heart. She intrigued him; she nurtured him. "I kept the romance quiet," he chuckled, "because neither of us wanted to talk about ourselves, except to ourselves."

He maintained the same level of privacy in all areas of life. It is a little known fact that he was an avid patron of the arts and a generous benefactor to beginning artists. He quietly provided the money necessary for many large art exhibits. One of the more prominent exhibitions being the 1938 Rochester, New York Memorial exhibition.

Producer Hunt Stromberg and MGM found another vehicle to present its singing sweethearts. This time, they decided to go all out. After "Girl of the Golden West", "the team" needed a fresh look. "Sweethearts" was to be MGM's first film shot entirely in technicolor. It was a whole new world for "the team" and they had a wonderful time.

It was the first time they had been filmed in modern dress. The added medium of color enhanced the warmth and realness of their personalities. The script allowed for a lot of joshing and fun with the MacDonald-Eddy personae. Also, they were provided the opportunity to sing more duets together than ever before---this film really presented "the team" in all their glory.

It was the first time Nelson and Jeanette appeared in color. The film portrays additional proof that when given the right script and atmosphere, Nelson and Jeanette could act and sing with joy, abandon and sparkle. "Sweethearts" stands today as one the best color films of its decade.

It was a reunion for Woody Van Dyke, Frank Morgan and the old gang. The pranks and clowning around permeated the set once again. "Sweethearts" was the outstanding money maker of 1938. Released around Thanksgiving, it became a holiday treat. The fans loved it. The "New York Times" termed it "a sumptuous Christmas package--a dream of ribbons, tinsel, technicolor and sweet theatrical sentimentality." Both Nelson's and Jeanette's abilities were enhanced by the fact that they were at one of the happiest period of their personal lives.

Nelson was at the height of his stardom, both personally and professionally. He was on top of the world. Often able to surpass the feats of others, Nelson's schedule for 1938-1939 defies belief. He performed 59 song recitals, 30 concerts, orchestra and oratorio dates, 65 radio shows, 8 opera performances, 28 special church services and made 3 major movies. In each instance, his fans were dazzled by his magnetism---he continued to emanate sincerity, humanness and dignity. In 1938, women rated their favorite film stars in this order: Nelson Eddy, Robert Taylor, Clark Gable, Bing Crosby and Deanna Durbin. He was the most popular entertainer on the radio in 1938 and 1939. The

Star of Stars picked, in order, Nelson Eddy, Edgar Bergen, Jack Benny and Don Ameche.

He often managed to squeeze in a brief visit to the family but Ginny remembers one particular visit more vividly than the others because so much happened.

> My mother was a strong woman---she never treated Nelson as though he were a special person. Mom knew Nelson loved a New England boiled dinner topped off with Indian Pudding covered with whipped cream. Once when he was performing in Boston, she offered to fix his favorite meal if he would stay over an extra night. Nelson was ecstatic! While she was in the kitchen preparing dinner, Nelson tried to get her goat and she kicked him out of the kitchen. She even scolded him for not coming to the table when dinner was ready. He had great respect for her and loved these special times.
>
> During these visits, he usually went to the attic to reminisce and look over his childhood things. On this particular evening while he was rummaging around the attic he found his favorite top. He brought it downstairs and announced to all of us that he was taking it back home with him.
>
> Time always went by all too quickly. When he was ready to leave the next day, Dad offered to drive him to the railroad station in Providence and I went along too. Nelson didn't like the exhaust smells that came from our old 1931 Buick and had Dad drive right then and there to the car dealer where he purchased a new 1938 Buick for us. Dad was thrilled of course, but I guess he was still in shock because when we returned home, he was white and Mom wanted to know what was wrong with him.

In 1939 he earned $6,000 a week from the Chase and Sanborn Hour except when he was touring. He earned

$18,000 annually from MGM for thirty weeks of work, and $20,000 a week from concerts he performed in approximately 20 weeks during the year. Add to that a tidy sum he got for his recordings and it all sounds quite nice. Then Uncle Sam came along to collect his due and Nelson went right back on concert tour. The reality of stardom is directly related to running a small business. Nelson was responsible for the economic welfare of his staff which included his manager, lawyers, accountant, secretary, voice teacher, accompanist, various consultants as well as his house staff.

When Nelson first arrived in Hollywood, he didn't know the first thing about acting. He never had done any and he certainly didn't know how to time lines, or to make gestures talk for him. He didn't know what a camera angle was. He had to be told how to do everything. Jeanette staggered him, because she never seemed to do anything wrong. Nobody had to tell her what to do or how to do it. Nelson used to wonder if it was just feminine instinct that told her, but now he knew from his own experiences that it was the practice, not only in the movies, but she had been on Broadway before that. He was ready to admit that he had suffered in those earlier years:

> I've never told anybody this before, I used to go through the tortures of the damned. I couldn't sleep at night for worrying about the next day's scene, about certain lines of dialogue that might throw me, or if certain bits of action didn't. I dreaded getting up in the morning, because once I was up the agony was just that much nearer. Every time I was called in front of the camera, I had a sinking sensation. Was this the time I wasn't going to be able to make the grade? I had to drive myself every inch of the way. I couldn't tell when I did something for the camera whether I

> was putting it over or not. I just had to rely on other people.

Finally, after six major film appearances, he was starting to relax and enjoy himself. He began to get the hang of it and was anxious for his next assignment. But he was also well aware that MGM gave him impossible roles to play which caused him to take a beating from the critics.

After the last successful pairing of "the team", Louis B. Mayer took a quick look at the profit line of "Sweethearts" and decided it was time to split his stars once again. Nelson's priority was his forthcoming marriage to Ann so he was easy to handle. Jeanette was also preoccupied as she was scheduled to leave on a concert tour. Also, Jeanette was not as pragmatic as Nelson. She knew they had a good thing going, but was equally interested in being recognized as a single celebrity, not always linked to "the team".

Nelson's new movie, "Let Freedom Ring", was an historical pageant. His co-star was Virginia Bruce. He loved having the opportunity to play a western lawyer and newspaperman who needed his fists as well as his brain to fight injustice in a small farming town. Nelson felt that if his movies didn't work out or the concerts dried up, he could return to another great love---newspaper work. He even had a major fight scene. It was a natural for him to portray his beliefs in truth and democracy. After the MacDonald-Eddy musicals, Nelson adapted remarkably well to this new screen image. Meanwhile, Jeanette filmed "Broadway Serenade" with Lew Ayres. Her plight with this movie was a mundane plot and some mixed signals in staging the finale by Busby Berkley. The film failed to click with the public.

Chapter Ten

Nelson and Ann felt they had waited long enough. He gave Ann a beautiful classic cut diamond ring in October of 1938. Sidney says it was a very romantic occasion. Still trying to carefully maintain their privacy, Ann wore the ring hidden beneath her white glove. But the privacy was soon to end.

Mr. and Mrs. Philip Denitz
have the honor of announcing
the marriage of their daughter
Ann Denitz Franklin
to
Mr. Nelson Eddy
on
Thursday, the 19th of January, 1939
Las Vegas, Nevada

Married by District Judge William E. Orr in his chambers, Nelson was 37, Ann 44. The ceremony was witnessed by Isabel, Doris Kenyon, and E.G. Osborn, Nelson's business manager. Ann glowed in a gray suit and an orchid corsage she wore for the occasion. Nelson was handsome as ever in a dark blue suit. His smile was likened to "the cat who swallowed the canary". So it was that America's most eligible bachelor, the love light in millions of women's eyes, lost his bachelor status to Ann Denitz Franklin. Nelson's devotion to Ann was well documented in Hollywood, so the marriage was not a surprise to any of Nelson's close associates. They had kept the relationship quiet out of respect for Nelson's and Ann's wishes.

For once Louella Parsons even held back the hottest gossip in town until after the elopement. She had previously hinted about the marriage, writing, "Nelson's car is parked at Ann Franklin's house so often, we bet it won't be long till its parked there for keeps." Nelson's popularity was so immense that the elopement was granted front page headlines across the country. Jeanette and Gene were the first to call, wanting to give them a party. The phone never stopped ringing as Hollywood extended its best to the newlyweds. Nelson was putting the finishing touches on "Let Freedom Ring" and a concert tour was scheduled to begin immediately, so the parties and congratulations were squeezed in between his commitments.

The marriage was obviously a shock to the millions of women who had deluded themselves into thinking Nelson could be theirs and they deplored the fact that Nelson had finally been captured. They made Ann the target of their disappointment. But Ann was ready for them. She was a very strong person. Instead of fighting them, she empathized with them and this seemed to help deaden the attacks. Nelson felt his marriage was a milestone for both of them. He was so "grateful for her." Ann, still disturbed by the millions of devoted fans, said, "May they forgive me for marrying Nelson and may they always remain faithful to him." Privately, the vehemence of their devotion frightened her.

Although the press continued to print outlandish stories about Nelson's love life, he ignored them---he remained mute. One reporter printed an article saying his marriage wasn't working out, while the newspaper across town wrote about the palatial honeymoon mansion they were building which had twenty-seven rooms. Other periodicals were busy reporting, "It's hush hush, but America's Singing Sweethearts are feuding" while their competition would headline, "America's Singing Sweethearts Happily Together Again."

Nelson and Ann decided to combine a honeymoon with Nelson's concert tour opening in Pasadena. They were then to go on to 30 cities including a special concert at the Metropolitan Opera in New York City and the Philadelphia Symphony, then on to Havana, Cuba. They would return in May to their new home which was in the process of being built. The headlines were absolutely out of sight. "Nelson Eddy Elopes January 20, 1939, " the Los Angeles Times wrote. Ann prepared herself for the hysterical attacks of the fans while the rumor mongers announced that Nelson's career was finished forever.

At the last minute, well meaning friends tried to tell Nelson that it was very bad business to try to take a honeymoon at the same time he was going on a concert tour. They admonished him that it would send chills into the hearts of all of his female admirers who constantly stormed the hotels and theaters, if he showed up with a wife. Nelson flatly refused to go unless Ann accompanied him, and furthermore, he refused to believe that any female admirer would be lost just because he got married. He truly believed that they loved his voice---not just him. So, after the ceremony, they spent a whopping twenty minutes at Boulder Dam alone before they started the tour.

The very first concert he performed as a married man made the next days paper. It seems that in the rush of things, Ann had forgotten to pack Nelson's suit vest. He put forth a frantic search for a substitute. He even solicited the audience for help, but to no avail. The audience long remembered how Nelson walked to the center of the stage and announced "this is going to be the most informal concert I ever gave. I'm going to introduce something new in evening wear." He then pointed to his middle and smiled sheepishly. The rest of his grey flannel suit was turned wrong side out with the ends tucked into his immaculate evening trousers. The audience loved it. The next morning, the Los Angeles Evening Herald & Express printed "Bride Forgets Vest" in bold block letters.

However, a few stops into the concert tour, Nelson and Ann realized they had a more serious problem. Ann, small and petite, had been jostled and almost trampled by the adoring fans, forcing Nelson to guard her with his body. He was livid! His little Annie would not be put through any more pain. The rules were immediately changed. No more Ann vying with the fans. By the eighth stop, the press was yelling where is Mrs. Eddy? Nelson, back in control, affable and handsome as ever, would talk about his concerts or his latest movie "Let Freedom Ring"; but when pushed, he set forth the new rule, "Mrs. Eddy never comes to interviews."

If that wasn't bad enough, the press criticized with more disparaging remarks, "Mrs. Eddy never, never has her picture taken with her husband."

Nelson pleaded, "Try to understand, the rule is privacy." From that point on Ann was rarely interviewed.

A gentleman of his word, he would protect his mate at all costs. Remember, he didn't choose some youthful glamor girl to marry and he had so far flaunted most of the accepted patterns for snaring Hollywood publicity. So why should this latest venture into marriage be different. In fact, it seemed to have increased his mystique rather than ruin it. When Ann did meet the press, the reporters described her as "a charming woman, with a fine sense of humor and piquant personality". Nelson received two million letters and telegrams congratulating him on his marriage. His reply, "I picked the best woman I could find."

When he married, everyone said his career was finished. They said he was every girl's dream man and no dream man could possibly marry and remain popular. But they were wrong. Women's Magazine chose Nelson Eddy as their favorite film star three years in a row. In April of 1939 his concert broke the house record, overflowing with 4500 music lovers.

The critics said he would lose his popularity, but they failed to consider three factors: Nelson's determination, his talent and tremendous charisma. Not only did his fans remain loyal but he added new fans to his admirers. There were subtle changes such as less foolishness and much less "isn't he adorable?" talk. Nelson was so relieved that he became friendly and relaxed once again. Millions of fans were glad to hear him return to the Chase and Sanborn Hour, and he received the 1939 Star of Stars Radio Award. He was stronger than ever---he was better than ever---he was happier than ever!

Nelson was noticeably different. He had wanted a home to share quiet evenings with Ann and Sidney. He wanted to be a good stepfather and provide comfort and warmth to his family. He was happy, relieved and at peace. But the rumors started to build momentum again. Louella Parsons printed a tasty bit of gossip about Nelson leaving his radio show which riled Nelson. "That's a pretty flight of fancy people are spreading around," Nelson said. "They are arguing about whether I lost my head or my voice." Actually he didn't lose either. The reasons for leaving were most logical. His new contract would keep him on the radio during the time he was to shoot a picture plus make several recordings. He would be right back on the same old treadmill. At thirty-eight, newly married and anxious to enjoy his new life, Nelson gave to his marriage what he had given to every important element in his life---always the

"Rose Marie"

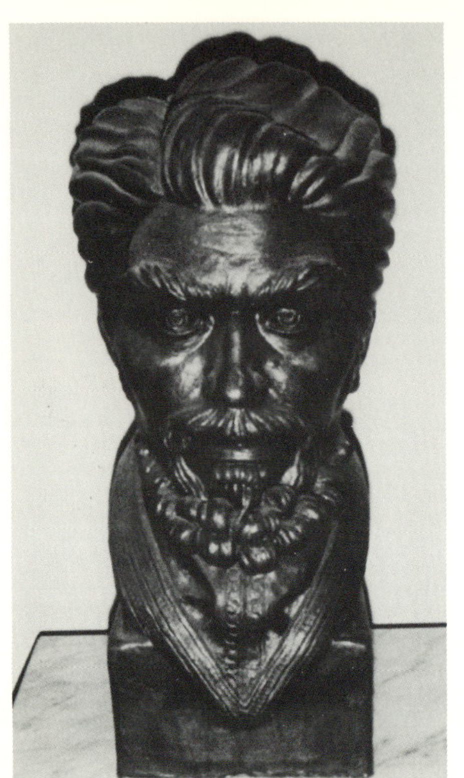

A Gift From Nelson Eddy

WILLIAM P. EDDY of Pawtucket, father of the movie and concert singer, admires a bronzed plaster head, "The Blind Plowman," which his son sent as a Christmas gift. The head was made by Nelson Eddy, who spends his leisure time sculpturing.

"Vassily" by Nelson from the "Chocolate Soldier"

Torso by Nelson

"Maytime"

"Chase and Sanborn Hour" Gang - NBC Radio

(Below) Mary Pickford, George Brent and wife Ruth Chatterton at Mrs. Sidney Franklin's party for Grace Moore, the blonde operatic star.

(Below) The Franklin party again. Lef to right, the hostess, Gloria and Mike Farmer, Grace Moore and Valentin Parerra, Carole Lombard and Bill Powell.

Ann Denitz Franklin - the hostess

Ann Denitz Eddy

Nelson

Ann's and Nelson's wedding picture

Isabel, Nelson, Ann, Doris Kenyon

"Ne-Top Farm", honeymoon home
"When I think how many songs I had to sing for it!" (Quote from back of photograph)

Honeymoon home as it looks today

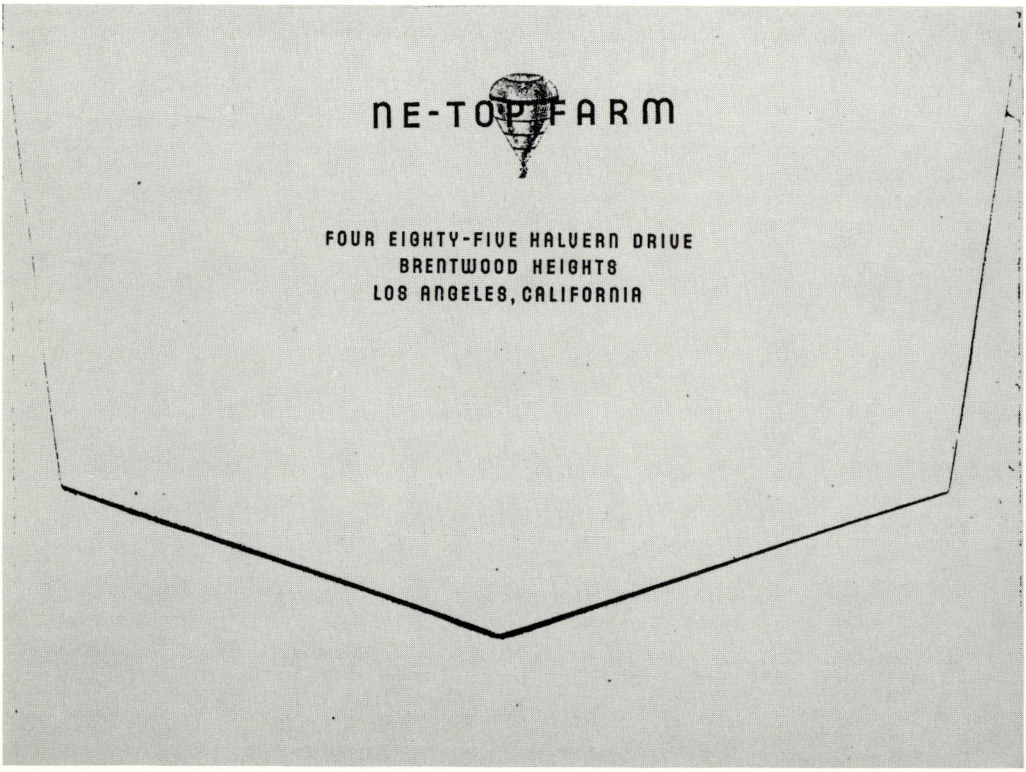

NE-TOP FARM

FOUR EIGHTY-FIVE HALVERN DRIVE
BRENTWOOD HEIGHTS
LOS ANGELES, CALIFORNIA

On the road

Nelson and Lily Pons in the backyard of Nelson's home

Nelson and Shirley Temple

Edgar Bergen, Charlie McCarthy, Nelson, Mae West and Bill Eddy

Ann and Isabel with Sheba and friend

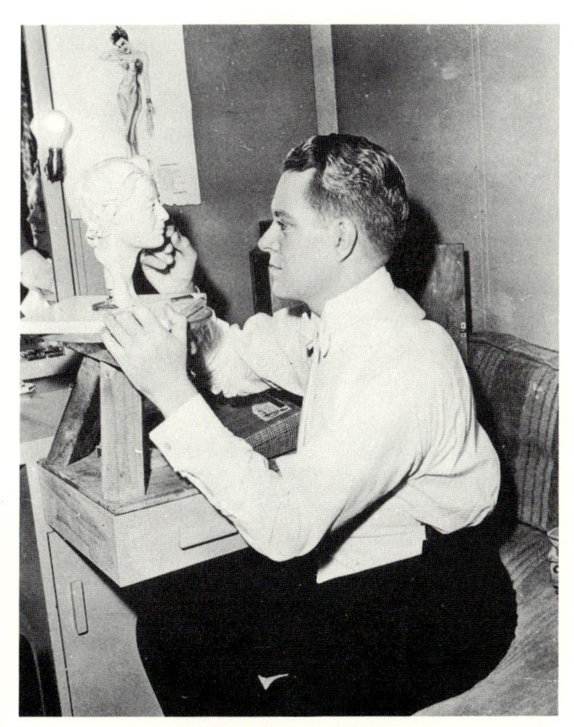

Nelson at work

Unfinished painting by Nelson

"*Sweethearts*"

Nelson and Buster

Sidney Jr. with his Chips (1941)

"Balalaika"

best. No contract was worth missing the little bit of home life he so desperately wanted and needed. His devotion to Ann had changed his priorities; he wanted to own his life for once. Nelson asked to be released from his contract with the Chase and Sanborn Hour. At the time he was one of the highest paid artists on radio. He was replaced by Donald Dickerson who received only one fourth of Nelson's salary. The Chase and Sanborn Hour was later cut to a half hour show.

Ann and Nelson had quietly looked for a home during the past year. They originally wanted a farm so they could plant crops. After months of looking, they were unable to locate a suitable site or even an established farm which they could call home. They did however discover four lots at the deadest end of a dead-end street in Brentwood. A quick visualization of their dream home was all it took. They purchased the property immediately.

The first thing Nelson did was to toss some vegetable seeds into the soil. He was ecstatic when the corn came up past his knees. For years Nelson's father had been writing to him about all the wonderful gardens he grew, raving about their successes. Nelson loved to work in the soil and was buoyed by the fact he had inherited some of his father's talent for gardening. Ginny also shared a love of gardening with Nelson. She remembers their common interest being their love of animals as well as their gardening talent.

Isabel remained in Nelson's old house in Beverly Hills. She loved the house so much that Nelson gave it to her. He and Ann would bicycle over to visit, swim or play tennis, since their new house had no pool or courts. Together they decided to surround their new home with beauty, not cement. Nelson and Ann landscaped their property with beautiful fruit trees, flowers, vegetable gardens and greenery.

Their new home on Halvern Drive adjoined the country estate of their friend Doris Kenyon Lasker, which is where Ann and Nelson had met five years before. Cesar Ramero and Robert Taylor lived around the corner. Nelson wanted to bring a little bit of his New England ancestry to Brentwood. The design was to be an exact replica of a Colonial home in Williamsburg, Virginia, not as large as people might imagine for a star of his standing. What people thought was of little importance to them. The house was magically evocative of Nelson's childhood. It also matched Ann's personality. Warm and inviting, with seven bathrooms and five bedrooms, it was utterly charming.

Nelson named his home "NETOP" farm. "NETOP" in Indian means "Welcome Friend", but the truer meaning was "Nelson Eddy's Top" --- his favorite childhood toy which he had found while rummaging through his father's attic. Marguerite even hooked him a rug with the top in the middle of it for their new home. Sidney recalled, "Nelson had a stable built because he had wanted to keep horses there but since there were no trails nearby where he could ride them, we kept chickens instead."

Built in 1939, at a cost of $47,000, Marston and Maybury were the architects and the contractor was C.E. Polikowski. One of the main focal points of their home was Nelson's music room. Dark woodwork trimmed the walls which held built-in breakfronts on either side of the fireplace. The domed ceiling was designed to enhance the perfect acoustics of the room.

Nelson and Ann devoted time to their love of antiques and filled their home with lovely pieces of furniture from their travels, along with heirlooms their parents and grandparents had passed down through the generations. Much of Nelson's art work was displayed throughout the house. Ann made sure that their home was comfortable in every way. Because Nelson was six foot two, the couches were extra long, the chairs were extra deep---the mattress was specially made. Everything was done to make Nelson's comfort the utmost priority.

Relaxed and settled, Nelson spent leisure time sculpting and painting. A natural sculptor, he began his work by carving his subjects from pieces of wood. He never sent his forms out to be fired or cast. Every detail was formed by his own hands. Bobby Armbruster has a magnificent horse's head sculpted by Nelson. He described Nelson's artistic technique in sculpturing as a perfect example of his character. Patience and modesty were his known attributes. Sidney expressed his solid agreement on the subject of Nelson's patience. He remembers Nelson working with him for hours upon end trying to teach him to model with clay. Nelson and Ann both wanted Sidney to sing. "I just couldn't sort out the languages. I didn't have the mind for it, but Nelson was a wonderful teacher. And then, when they saw how easily mathematics and science came to me---that was that."

Nelson believed that nothing had come easily and he always put forth effort in the beginning of any task, working consistently towards its end so that he could enjoy the final result. He studied anatomy for two years to improve the intricate posturing of the human body. He was very modest about his talent, but his friends were far more verbal. He was an exceptional artist and used many mediums to display his talents. Much of his artwork is intact today and deeply valued by his friends. He took great pride in his work. He was very prolific---there were many recipients of his talents. He gave Jeanette a beautiful oil painting of herself, as well as a detailed bust. He sculpted a bust of Woody Van Dyke. His co-stars were often given personalized pieces of his art work.

All of Nelson's old friends were always welcome at the Eddy's. Some of the socializing changed a bit because now he was part of a couple, but all his friends stayed intact. He became his old self. He got kind of a bang out of life, including his marriage. He loved horses and began to educate himself about them. He went back to being the extrovert. It was as if someone pulled the plug and he was released. But he would not talk about his marriage. "Why make me self-conscious at home," he would demand. "Ann is not an actress, so the less publicity she has, the happier she'll be and I'm out to make her happy one hundred per cent." While Nelson and Ann were setting up housekeeping as the perfect couple of 1939, the fans remained confused but steadfastly loyal.

Life at home encompassed all the joys and tribulations of family life. Sidney was fifteen years old when Nelson and Ann married. A typical teenager, he was rebellious and content to go his own way while marking out his independence. There is no doubt that Sidney caused his mother a great deal of pain during those years. As Sidney describes it, "she was always waiting for the other shoe to fall."

Nelson had other ideas; it was obvious some adjustments had to be made. Sidney remembers those days well. "Nelson was a strict disciplinarian and I was a troublesome, dumb kid," he smiled. "I wanted to continue to run around nights with my friends from Beverly Hills High School and Nelson laid down rules and standards. It wasn't the easiest of times. But there were some great moments."

Sidney was still attending Beverly Hills High School when he asked permission to invite a girl friend home for dinner. Ann and Nelson were delighted. The young woman Sidney invited for dinner in 1939 is known today as

June Haver, the actress. In his excitement, Sidney left out one important piece of information---he forgot to tell June that his step-father was the one-and-only Nelson Eddy. She walked in and was overwhelmed to hear Nelson offer to take her on a guided tour of their home. "He was utterly charming," remembers June. "He showed me the rose garden and told me how much he loved flowers and working in the yard. He took me to the music room and showed me a bust that he had just finished. It was a gorgeous sculpture of Jeanette MacDonald." June and Sidney didn't date much after that, but June still remembers that wonderful visit to this very day. It would be ten years before June and Nelson would meet again regarding this very special house.

Chapter Eleven

As a young star on the MGM lot during Nelson's era, Kathryn Grayson reminisced about those times and her relationship with Nelson:

> He was one of three people that helped the young stars at MGM. The other two were Jeanette MacDonald and Joan Crawford. Nelson wowed all the young girls. Under Louis B. Mayer you had to be a gentlemen whether you were or not; but Nelson was the exception, because he really was. All the young singers loved him. Nelson's voice was one of the most lasting voices I have ever heard. He was happiest when he sang. He sang beautifully till the day he died.

In recalling Nelson's relationship with Jeanette, Kathryn emphasized:

> If ever there were disagreements, of which I doubt, they were what you described in show business as "creative disagreements". Nelson was funny, loving and warmhearted. He loved the companionship of people. We were family back then; we took our talent seriously and gave our best. We respected each other and those qualities carried over into our friendships. Those of us who remain today are still close.

As a profit-making star, MGM knew they could count on Nelson to bring in a good return. Once again he was separated from Jeanette. This time, he would star with Ilona Massey in "Balalaika". MGM wanted to present Ilona to her fullest advantage and Nelson was the perfect co-star to assist her.

"Balalaika" portrays Nelson at his very best. Relaxed and at ease, he and Ilona convey great warmth via the screen. Nelson, the linguist, had already taught himself to speak fluent Russian. His role as a Russian prince falling in love with a Bolshevik revolutionary evokes a tale of social significance. The film includes songs such as *Volga Boatman, Toreador Song* from "Carmen" and the title song, *At the Balalaika*. Nelson's version of *Silent Night* sung in German is one of his most emotion filled renderings on film.

Another factor which contributed to his new image was his feelings for Ilona Massey. He was very fond of her and is credited with helping her become a movie star. The press had a heyday with Nelson's more relaxed image on the screen. After some forethought, he interviewed for the press with the following:

> So I'm freer and easier. I'll tell you one answer. In "Balalaika", I wore some pants that wouldn't split if I bent over. Don't think that didn't make a difference! Some of the musical comedy uniforms I've had to wear have been brutal. Pants so tight I couldn't sit down without courting catastrophe. Coats so wasp-waisted I couldn't take a deep breath without having sixteen buttons pop off. Collars so high I had to hold my chin just one way---up at a forty-five degree angle. People said Eddy was stiff. And how Eddy was stiff!
>
> In "Balalaika", I wore Cossack clothes which were designed for comfort. I relaxed a little. I forgot to worry for the first time since I came to Hollywood. I stopped knocking myself out trying to act. I had three and a half days off in three months---and I put on ten pounds. I was that relaxed. I don't know. Maybe that makes me a new Eddy.

The "new Eddy" was very busy with other facets of his career and it didn't go unnoticed. In June of 1939, the American Institute of Cinematography bestowed upon Nelson the Award of Achievement and an honorary membership in recognition of his distinguished contribution in advancing the standards of musical interpretation in motion pictures. He was elected "Star of Stars" in Radio Guide's poll, and on October 19th, he was the honored guest star with Leopold Stokowski in a Los Angeles concert for Polish War Relief. It was his first in a long line of war benefit performances.

"The team" had always been extremely popular in Europe and remain so to this day. But as the winds of war began blowing across the continent, changes were imminent. Eleven countries chose to close their theaters to English speaking movies. Dark clouds spread across the sky as America was about to be thrust into a world of war and destruction. The country was soon to face the harsh realities of the oncoming conflict.

Other unsettling issues were facing "the team" much closer to home. The studio gave them old plots and rehashed versions of other films, but failed to develop new material for them. Both Nelson and Jeanette were past the age of playing young characters, starry-eyed and vibrant. Nelson pointed out, "I'm no longer a jumping juvenile". These disturbing elements combined to set the stage for "the team's" downfall.

Chapter Twelve

Nelson may have played a romantic on the screen, but in real life he was an unflappable realist. While the monolithic studios and their powerful icons held on tight, Nelson quietly pulled back to walk his solitary path; it was time for him to re-evaluate. He had choices, but they had to be studied very carefully.

He invested cautiously to protect his future because he understood the fleeting existence of stardom. He watched as others around him squandered their quickly earned wealth. Hollywood was a make believe kingdom where it was easy to become caught up in the over abundance of material opulence. He readily admitted that his fame afforded him a quality of life he truly enjoyed. He knowingly spoiled Ann because he wanted the very best for her. But it was a conservative life style when compared to the affluence of other stars. Still, the dilemma remained. Even though he worked hard and spent his money wisely, he had to maintain consistent earnings in order to protect his assets. Once you lost your place in the contrived cast system that Hollywood, the fan magazines and the general population supported, you also lost your life style.

He spent a great deal of time contemplating the path down which his movie stardom had taken him. Neither he nor Jeanette were happy with the choices MGM had made for them. Both were known to argue vehemently with the studio bosses but to no avail. The studio always won. Nelson suffered the outcome of the studio's choices even more than Jeanette because his screen image had never been a positive one. When the critics would plummet him with their latest reviews, the embarrassment was doubly hard for him to swallow. Many of the stars questioned the studio's hard core methods and while the disruptive voices were heard within the studio power structure, the country was becoming more and more immersed in the chaos shaking Western Europe. Fear slowly seeped into the minds and hearts of people where complacency had once comfortably existed.

Nelson never lost his passion for opera. It had once sorely tempted him with its majestic presence, but he passed it by because of his own inner doubts. Moreover, he recognized that for all its glory only forty thousand people could be reached in one season while the motion picture screen could reach sixty to eighty million. Nothing could change that critical fact. Nelson deeply loved his fans and the mass exposure that the movie screen afforded him.

He had reached the pinnacle of his career. Considered to be the best lyric baritone of the century, he knew he was blessed. For twenty years he tirelessly performed before thousands, while striving to constantly improve himself. But instead of resting on his laurels, he strove even harder for perfection. Rather than take advantage of his fame, he chose instead to give something back to those who believed in him. Thousands of struggling young singers clamored for his advice and guidance. Regardless of his contract agreements, concert tours and personal concerns, and because of his own painful memories, he still felt compelled to help them. Even if young singers didn't make it, he tried to give them the needed strength to try.

Nelson remembered vividly how the neighbors complained of his bellowing and how hard he had worked to add the dramatic quality to his voice which he felt was so sorely lacking. He never got over the fact that, all during his long struggle, no one but his family truly believed in his talent. It had taken such prolonged efforts to color his voice with humility, imagination and dreams; it seemed an eternity. Because of his own experiences, he was always hesitant to postulate about his expertise. After all, most of the advice which had been given to him had proven to be detrimental. He told one young singer,

> There is needed in our creative genes an added ingredient which gives us the ability to strive forward, to push on and never stop trying. Talent and training aren't enough without this tremendous power. It took years of study to attain greatness. A career in opera might involve fifteen years of constant study. If you can master Mozart, you can sing anything, but the most difficult for me is the German Lieder.

He often performed at religious services throughout the Los Angeles area. Stardom was never an issue when it came to helping other young singers. In one particular situation, Nelson actually ended up singing in the church choir at the Beverly Hills Episcopalian Church just so a talented young tenor could receive the proper audition. The choir director had filled his schedule with stiff competition for the tenor part, but Nelson's young acquaintance had no portfolio to present when he requested his audition and therefore the director turned him away. When Nelson offered to compensate the director's time by performing at his church, the director acquiesced. No one was more elated than Nelson when the young tenor was eventually chosen for the part.

Sometimes Nelson was confused by his fans. "Perhaps the audiences prefer that singers perform only within the limits of their understanding". He began to wonder if it was the popular music or the arias which people really wanted from him.

His solicitous behavior often created humorous results. In 1940, John Carroll made his movie debut in a film called "High Gaucho". John had trouble singing *The Song of the Open Road* which was a well-known choice of Nelson's concert repertoires. John came to Nelson for help in learning to sing the song correctly so Nelson recorded the song on his recording machine and John practiced along with Nelson's voice. John was so enchanted by the complex recording machine that he begged Nelson to sell it to him. In the end, Nelson hung on to his prized machine, but John got the last laugh when the movie premiered. As Nelson watched, John appeared on the screen riding horseback and singing *The Song of the Open Road,* a la Nelson.

Even at the height of his success, his penchant for perfection meant continuous training in both voice and diction. He never altered his level of intense study regardless of his other commitments and he often wrote articles on proper training and voice techniques for professional singers. He recorded his concert favorites, operatic arias, hymns, carols, folk songs, love ballads, sea shanties, humorous songs, lieder, popular ballads, western-style, spirituals, etc. He often recorded in various languages, and with a variety of well-known artists, including Jeanette MacDonald, Dorothy Kirsten, Eleanor Steber, Jo Stafford, Theodore Paxson, Rise Stevens and Nadine Connor. The highest praise that can be paid any recording artist is that he is a musician as well as a performer. When Nelson decided to record two Stephen Foster albums, he didn't just pick out the well-known Foster favorites. Instead, he studied the complete life of Stephen Foster and every one of his lesser-known songs, before making his choices.

Nothing soured his good natured personality quicker than reading a few distorted stories about his life or family. He was quick to anger when exploited or besmirched.

More often than not, he was deeply hurt because he couldn't understand nor accept the mentality of those who twisted the truth. He remained honest and direct in his dealings with the press. Many times, he was too honest for his own good.

There were many frustrations in Nelson's life at this time. Life was no longer as smooth as he had hoped---so much was out of his control. While the country teetered on the brink of war, the clouds surrounding his career also grew darker.

Sidney Junior had just turned sixteen. As a bright, rebellious young boy, he fit the description of an exasperating teenager perfectly. Parenting a teenager was very foreign to Nelson, but he tried hard to slow Sidney down. So did Ann and Sidney's father, but none of them knew what to expect next from their crafty teenager.

On one occasion, Sidney had just passed his drivers test. He immediately did what any newly licensed teenager would do---he asked Nelson if he could borrow the family car for a high school dance. Unwilling to relinquish the car, Nelson offered to drive Sidney and his date. After a minor battle, needless to say, Nelson won! When Nelson and Sidney arrived to pick up Sidney's date---you can imagine Sidney's chagrin when his prized date took one look at Nelson Eddy and announced, "If you don't mind Sidney, I think I'd like to ride up front with the chauffeur!" Nelson loved it, but begrudgingly admitted that Sidney deserved the chance to take the car on his own.

So when the next big date arrived, Nelson gave Sidney the car. Ann sat up until 1:00 in the morning worrying while the clock ticked away the minutes. Around 2:00, the phone rang and Nelson and Ann reacted with immediate dread. Their fears were confirmed as Sidney excitedly explained he had had an accident. He had hit a car at a stop sign, but he assured them there were no injuries.

The events that followed caused Nelson and Ann great alarm. It turned out that Sidney hit the car of a young actress. Her lawyer suggested she sue Nelson, for he had plenty of money. After the initial shock, Nelson became philosophical. "It's good to get shaken up every now and then because its makes you a little more cautious," he explained to Sid. The case eventually went to trial and the Eddys were found "not guilty". Sidney drove very slowly for a long time to come.

Chapter Thirteen

Eighteen months had passed since Jeanette and Nelson had been together and the fans were clamoring loudly for a reunion of their "singing sweethearts". The studio chose Robert Z. Leonard's "New Moon", a Sigmund Romberg romantic comedy, for their next film. It was to be released in 1940. Originally performed in 1930 by Lawrence Tibbett and Grace Moore, it had been a highly successful endeavor. But the old saying "if it works, don't fix it" didn't hold true for Nelson and Jeanette's version of "New Moon". Once again, MGM stepped in and began altering the plot. They proceeded to drop several of the original songs which only marred the original beauty of the story even more. What could have been a delightful light-hearted operetta was turned into a mediocre film and once again it was at the expense of Nelson and Jeanette's screen image.

It was a strain on both stars to maintain an aura of freshness while trying to work with such a diluted film score. Fed up as they already were, they became even more candid in their frustrations when the film was finally released. The audiences liked "New Moon" well enough, but the press made sure to stress the point that "New Moon" in no way possessed the magnetism of the old MacDonald/Eddy movies. Both Nelson and Jeanette realized that the romantic glossy operettas of the past had seen better days, not just for them but for everyone.

America was out of the maudlin depression era. Times had changed. "Gone With the Wind" was a box office smash and it was clear to all that audiences were responding to a new type of hero and heroine. Still the studio refused to listen to them as their cries fell on deaf ears.

Even the New York Times prophesied the future for Nelson and Jeanette:

> Somehow the familiar lilt of the old MacDonald-Eddy extravaganzas is missing from this "New Moon". Both the principals still give with all the winsome but slightly ponderous charm they possess in the dramatic interludes...but it never quite comes alive...With tears wallowing in our eyes...we rather sadly suspect that this sort of sugar-coated musical fiction has seen its better days.

Why MGM didn't sit up and take note of what was happening is beyond the realm of imagination. Perhaps they were just blind or overly sentimental. The future did not bode well for Nelson and Jeanette and no one realized it more than they did.

Back on the home front, a family meeting was called to discuss the dilemma of Sidney Junior. In matters relating to his step-son, Nelson always gave his opinion and then deferred the final decision to Ann and Sidney Senior. Sidney explained:

> My father and Nelson had a good relationship, they were both artists; Dad's media being watercolor. They also were avid readers and enjoyed discussing everything from art to barbecuing. In the case of sending me away to school - it was definitely my mother and father who decided to enroll me in Webb Preparatory School in Claremont, California, for the benefit of peace at home. They felt I needed a more structured educational environment. I hated it - I rebelled like hell, but it didn't do a bit of good and off I went.

Nelson tried to relax and prepare for his next concert tour. He was always happiest when singing for his multitude of fans, and the fans were always happiest when close to their idol. Hundreds of his devoted fans followed him from city to city during his concert tour. Then they would gather to postulate on what Nelson was <u>really</u> like. Many of the fans drew attention to the large number of suitcases Nelson carried when he traveled. Only his family and close friends knew that he carried a traveling library with him on tour. For instance, at the beginning of his concert tour in 1946, he started studying Spanish, and after twenty-six stops, spoke it fluently! Often times he would carry plaster, easel, brushes and paints in his suitcase and work on his sculpture and painting after a performance.

During this particular concert tour, he was growing increasingly concerned about the rumor that he was losing his eye-sight. He began to grow fearful that the rumor might even diminish his career. Only two weeks earlier while performing at the Mosque Theater, he had had a rather frightening experience. He was taking a bow before 4,000 people when suddenly an attractive young woman climbed onto the stage and advanced towards him. Nelson headed for the wings as the stagehands intercepted her. She explained that upon hearing that Nelson was going blind, she merely wanted to pin a religious medal on him.

Now, when he read the latest headlines "Nelson Eddy is Going Blind", he became furious. Right then and there, he stalked down to the "Kansas City Times" and solicited their help in dispelling the false rumors. The reporters were concerned as well over the libelous stories and responded by immediately printing an article entitled "A Hoax Follows Eddy". "All I know is that for the last couple of years the world has been going around saying I'm going blind. Maybe it's because I wear dark glasses, but then, so does everybody else in Hollywood. I used to have trouble with the klieg lights on the set, but I have since learned how to work under them."

In the quiet of his hotel room, Nelson finally unraveled the mystery of the rumors source. He always carried a little black book in his hands while singing on stage. It contained all of his lyrics and he felt it was a graceful device to hold in his hands rather than let his arms hang stiffly by his side. *The Blind Ploughman* was included in every concert repertoire. This song had special meaning to him because he believed the song conveyed a message of inspiration to all who heard it. While singing the song, he would become very serious and stare intensely above the heads of the audience. He never for one moment realized that this dramatic rendering of the song made him appear to the audience as though he were blind.

He was so distraught by the rumor that he called on his old friend Louella Parsons to help him out. Louella loved Nelson and prided herself in their friendship. The following day she wrote in her column, "Thank heavens now that Nelson Eddy fans throughout the country can see for themselves that he's not blind, Nelson can leave on the three-month concert tour which opens in Sacramento and do justice to what he does best---sing." At his very next appearance, Nelson made sure to change his stance and eye contact while singing *The Blind Ploughman* and, for added measure, he chose something slightly humorous to sing next so that the serious mood would be counteracted. The rumor slowly died, but it remained a strong reminder to Nelson that his career was a very fragile commodity indeed.

The only rumor that Nelson could never dispel centered around his marriage to Ann. It was often written that he couldn't possibly have a good marriage to anyone because he was never home. Although the rumor pained him, only once did he complain publicly, "It has always been a mystery to me how Bob Hope for example can travel his entire life, yet no one utters a word about his marriage being in trouble." Nelson can be faulted for doing nothing to combat the rumors or defend his position, but he and Ann both felt it would only put more demands on their privacy. Eventually, they learned to live with the rumors rather than fight them.

Nelson and Jeanette continued in their separate endeavors hoping against all hope for things to improve at MGM. It wasn't long before MGM called them back to the studio. W.S. Van Dyke who had directed "Naughty Marietta" and "Rose Marie" was going to rejoin "the team" in the film "Bittersweet". This time MGM was going to do better by their stars or so they promised.

"Bittersweet" was Noel Coward's beautiful romantic story of life in old Vienna. The studio even decided to splurge and film "the team" in technicolor to show them good faith. Although the studio captured Nelson and Jeanette's trust for a short period of time, it was not to last. Shortly after the filming began, the studio returned to their old ways and began to rewrite the beginning and end of the movie. As they tore the script apart, they tried to calm Nelson and Jeanette by explaining that the story line was too similar to "Maytime". But nothing the studio did changed the similarity to "Maytime" nor enhanced the script for its frustrated actors. Even the critics hailed "Bittersweet as a repeat. In the film, Nelson is shot and dies in less than three seconds. This became the quickest death scene ever enacted on the movie screen. Nelson and Jeanette knew the outcome of this film before it even premiered. Unfortunately for their millions of fans and for the studio itself, "Bittersweet" was the first financial failure of the MacDonald/Eddy team.

Jeanette was now thirty-seven and Nelson thirty-nine. They were too old to play these make-believe parts any longer. Nelson continued his tremendously successful concert tours, while Jeanette searched for new avenues to continue her professional career. It appeared to critical observers that MGM had under their wings the two top commercial entertainers of an era and felt that their popularity alone could carry them regardless of the vehicle that they were given to act in. Rather than provide them with new scripts, new ideas and new creative endeavors, the studio chose to consistently star them in the remakes of older films. This was a grievous error, not only for Nelson and Jeanette, but for Louis B. Mayer as well.

Chapter Fourteen

According to their family and close friends, Ann's influence on Nelson was profound. Sidney recalls that their personalities were beautifully matched. Both were cultured and sophisticated people; Nelson self-taught and Ann raised with the refinement which belies a lady. Their time together was spent reading, visiting the famous museums and art galleries during Nelson's concert tours and entertaining small groups of friends in their home. They called each other by endearing nicknames and their shared intimacies included private notes written only for each others eyes. Nelson was quick to tell those close to him that Ann was his severest critic and his most avid supporter. He trusted her judgement implicitly. Ann knew and understood Nelson's need for challenges. She encouraged the challenges and Nelson thrived on them.

He voraciously worked crossword puzzles and played solitaire. He and Ann played gin rummy with a win or die mentality. When something was too much for him or he got bogged down with his scripts, he would transfer his efforts to a crossword puzzle, painting or sculpture. Then without a word, he would return to the problem at hand and quietly resolve the dilemma without losing a beat.

His newest hobby was horses. He had always loved animals and California provided the perfect climate for his love of the outdoor life. He was wealthy enough to pursue his life long love of horses and quickly became an avid horseman. He owned and groomed his own horses and whenever they could, he and Ann would ride into the hills surrounding Los Angles.

He became a contributing author to "Equestrian Magazine". One of his funniest articles was about a horse named Ida and he entitled it, "I Bought A Horse". It was a priceless bit of commentary about his stubborn determination to ride a rather tenaciously skittish horse named Ida.

Whenever Nelson mounted Ida, she would perform an up and down roller coaster movement in the hopes of dismounting him. It was a fight from beginning to end with man pitted against animal. Ann entered the picture out of concern for Nelson's well being. Visions of Nelson lying sprawled and broken somewhere were not at all to her liking so she decided to join Nelson on a trail ride. Ann rode her own trusted mount, Donna, while Nelson rode Ida. All was going well when Ida began to do her "roller coaster ride". Ida would go up and down trying to throw Nelson off.

Ann took one look at these shenanigans and began to rant and rave, "Listen here, I love you, and if anything should happen to you, I'd die. That 'she devil' could pitch you off onto a hard spot and break your neck."

Nelson got a kick out of Ann's ravings and decided to try and prove her wrong. He chided her, "Oh, you're just jealous Ann" and cantered off sideways into a hedge. He absolutely refused to give Ida up, trying every new trick in the book to get the horse to cooperate with him. Then one day, Ida charged at Nelson and it really shook him up. He decided to have her checked because obviously something was very wrong and that's when he discovered that Ida was with child. He scolded himself for forcing her to carry him when he should have just left her out in the pasture. Unwilling to risk life and limb again, he bade Ida farewell.

Nelson loved his horses and they provided many a humorous story as well as long hours of enjoyment for the

Eddys. His favorite horse was "Ebony", a saddle bred show ring horse whom Nelson rode Western style and used in his movies. They rode the bridle trails of Griffith Park and Providencia Ranch. They were often joined on the trails by their close friends, particularly Elinor and Wayne Griffin.

Nelson originally came to know Elinor Griffin in 1937 through her music. Elinor, known internationally as Elinor Remick Warren, is an American composer who has written choral works and instrumental compositions for many years. Nelson had sung Elinor's song *My Parting Gift* during a concert in Los Angeles. Feeling that he had failed to do her song justice, he wrote her a letter of apology. "After doing so poorly with your song, I feel ashamed to face you. I think I can get a hold of it and eventually make it go," he explained. From that time on, they were close friends and he often visited her to discuss musical compositions. Elinor frequently commented that Nelson was far too critical of his own musical talent. Elinor's husband, Wayne Griffin, the producer of "The Burns and Allen Show", also became one of Nelson's closest confidants. Both couples chose to remain apart from the Hollywood social scene. Elinor and Wayne were close friends of the Raymonds and the Gables as well.

Jeanette's and Nelson's repertoires included many of Elinor Warren's songs, among them *Heather* and *Down in the Glen*. Nelson loved to sing Elinor's *Remembering* and *Sweet Grass Range.* One year while on tour, the Eddy's found an antique mug which they presented to Elinor. On it was an anonymous English poem about gardening which she used as the text for the song *To The Farmer* composed especially for Nelson. Their friendship would continue throughout their lives.

While Nelson was on concert tour, Jeanette launched an all out war on MGM to let her make a film with her husband, Gene Raymond. This time, she pulled out all the stops and, reluctantly, MGM acquiesced and gave them the script for the remake of "Smilin' Through".

Meanwhile the country was celebrating the election of a new Democratic president. Nelson, accompanied by Ted, sang at the Inaugural Gala for Franklin D. Roosevelt on January 19, 1941 at Constitution Hall. Also on the program were Douglas Fairbanks, Raymond Massey, Charles Chaplin, Mickey Rooney and Metropolitan Opera mezzo-soprano Rise Stevens. Nelson teased that, although he was a Republican, a job was still a job.

While Jeanette was making "Smilin' Through", Nelson returned home exhausted but exhilarated from his tour. MGM didn't wait long before calling him back to the studio to co-star with Rise Stevens in the movie "Chocolate Soldier". It would be Rise's film debut and she was very excited. Rise was enthusiastically received when she sang at the Metropolitan Opera and this was a new opportunity to expand her career. Nelson finished his concert tour just in time to start filming in April. In his naivete he was quoted as saying, "I really think the fans are finally getting more sensible about separating Jeanette and I. I use to get the most indignant letters scolding MGM anytime there was talk of our parting." Nelson may well have thought that was the way it was, but he was quickly to be proven wrong. The press referred to Rise as the girl who took Jeanette MacDonald's place. Even the dresses she wore in the film had originally been designed for Jeanette. This made the comparison between the two even more pronounced. Rise was never able to remove herself from Jeanette's shadow, and it was to prove disastrous for her.

Nelson, however, scored a double success. First, he proved himself an "adept farceur in a risque comedy" displaying aptly his ability for comedy as well as mimicry in the dual role as husband and lover. The critics gave him critical acclaim for his remarkable impersonation of the Russian lover, Vassily, as well as for his rendition of the bass aria *The Song of the Flea.* Columnist Jimmy Fidler gave Nelson a "best performance" rating for his role by stating, "A great singer proves he's become a fine actor."

Nelson sighed in relief, but even with the plaudits, he knew he was doomed at MGM. Without efforts to enhance his roles there would be little opportunity to survive. Rise Stevens gave a fine performance but suffered from the critical reviews. Before returning to her first love, the Metropolitan Opera, she made two more films, "Going My Way" and "Carnegie Hall" which the critics applauded .

The "sweetheart years" were coming to an end. The old fashioned romance we had clung to was being swept away by the realities of war. The sweet sentimentality of the 1930's was now being drowned out by the roaring sound of machine gun artillery. It seemed as if overnight the age of innocence had vanished.

On June 27th, 1941, Nelson stood among 1600 members of the regular graduating class to receive a Master of Music Degree at the University of Southern California. He received the honorary degree for his work in films and on the concert stage. He was always a little reticent about his education and the degree meant a great deal to him because he had been self-taught. That same year the National Federation of Music Clubs named him the Best Male Singer of the Year at their Los Angeles Convention.

Nelson was still raging a battle at MGM. At one point, he had the opportunity to star in a non-singing film with Louise Rainer, but MGM refused to break his contract. Not long after that fiasco, Warner Brothers solicited him for "Desert Song", but MGM refused again. They held him to his contract and starred him in the doomed film, "I Married An Angel", with Jeanette.

Once again MGM promised Nelson and Jeanette that all would be well. "I Married An Angel" was released in 1942. It was to be the last film Jeanette and Nelson would ever make together. Their old friend Woody Van Dyke, now a major in the army, agreed to direct the film, but even his efforts were thwarted.

The original plan had been to use "I Married An Angel" for Jeanette in 1933. The studio rejected the idea because the plot suggested wanton amorality. It worked beautifully when Rogers and Hart brought it to Broadway in 1938. But the usually impressive production numbers staged by MGM were curtailed because of wartime restrictions and the material itself was so poorly scripted that Nelson and Jeanette didn't have a chance. In the end, they were duped into a useless attempt to save the film.

Nelson pulled off the part of a rich banker, the dashing Count Willie, who is surrounded by women while Jeanette plays the sweetly innocent stenographer turned angel who, in Willie's dream, marries him. Both stars should be given credit for their efforts, but the film offered them little romance, no duets and terrible lines. To keep his sanity, Nelson sculptured the two statues which can be seen in the early scenes taken inside the bank.

It was Louis B. Mayer's decision and his alone that caused this films failure. Neither Nelson nor Jeanette were suited for these parts and each loudly opposed making the film. Their vocal abilities were never utilized and the critics could barely find any merit in the script, staging direction, or musical score.

Jeanette and Nelson had previewed the film on "Hollywood Radio Theater" on June 1, 1942, but they themselves knew they were beaten. Nelson provided a very good burial for "I Married An Angel".

> In our films together Jeanette and I always depicted pure love and we had a lot of trouble with this script because most religions disapproved of an angel going to bed with a man. Everybody on the lot told us either it was going to be the best picture we ever did or the worse. Well, it was the worse. It took the studio years to decide how to present it without offending anybody and when they did, they slashed it to pieces. When we finally finished, it was a horrible mess.

Nelson was understandably angry with MGM. He was disheartened, depressed and tired of fighting a useless battle with Louis B. Mayer. He had never had an agent before, but he hired Leland Hayward, the producer turned agent, to negotiate his release from MGM. Leland was unsuccessful in negotiations and Nelson finally stepped in to take control. As he so aptly put it, "The first time I ever hired an agent and it cost me my career." It also cost him $50,000 in cash to break his contract and walk out of MGM a free man. It was a painfully expensive lesson, but in July, 1942, he walked a little taller and a little prouder.

In September, the Academy Award for best picture went to MGM's "Mrs. Miniver" which was produced by Sidney Franklin Sr. Both having experienced the ire of Louis B. Mayer, Nelson and Sidney were quite surprised but gratified to hear a somewhat humbled Mayer admit to the audience that it was Sidney who indeed deserved the honor.

Chapter Fifteen

The "Electric Hour" was a perfect replacement for Nelson's time and energy. With Bobby Armbruster as musical director and talented guest stars to sing duets with every week, his outlook brightened. Ann made sure to attend the broadcasts often, but always remained out of the limelight. This was Nelson's dream show because it had a musical format. Bobby's memory of "The Electric Hour" is that it was "an awful lot of fun". As soon as the station announced Nelson's show, the women came in droves to the recording studio. But once they were seated, his fans were models of proper decorum. Nelson's career had many facets, but he loved the concertizing and radio shows the best.

Bobby Armbruster remarked:

> People don't understand the fun of those days. The shows were less like work than anything I've ever done, because we really enjoyed ourselves. We had such fun and we were friends---good friends. If Nelson's critics were quick to say he was stiff and awkward as an actor, nothing could mask his personal charisma, the masculine appeal, polish and intelligence that emanated from him in person.

Some of Nelson's best music was performed on "The Electric Hour" which was broadcast from 1942 to 1946. The network gave Nelson and Bobby total control over the choice of music and songs used on the show. Nelson chose to sing serious arias such as those from Boris Godunof. He entwined the light lyrical with classical and the musical mix proved as successful over the air-waves as it had been in his concerts. Nelson, Bobby, the announcer and guest stars would meet a few days before air time to go over the orchestrations and layout.

As Bobby Armbruster stated:

> I have accompanied hundreds of singers throughout my professional life, but feel that Nelson was by far the best musician. During my long and close association with him, Nelson never lost his temper or mistreated anyone in my presence. Serious in his desire for perfection, he was always gentle towards others while reaching for his goal. Nelson and I shared the same philosophy, and it helped us through those years in Hollywood. We had this attitude that said, all this will be over and we'll still be around so just hang in there.

Unfortunately Nelson didn't make it, but Bobby did. Today he and Don Ameche go to the same doctor. Bobby is so proud of Don's successes. "It does my heart good." Nelson and Bobby agreed that Don Ameche had the greatest laugh around---he just wishes Nelson was still here to laugh with them. Bobby was 93 when I interviewed him in October of 1989; he was sprightly, charming and very much at peace with the world. When I last saw him, he was plotting how to renew his driver's license.

Norma McDaniel was the original script girl on "The Electric Hour" from 1942 to 1946 and Nelson Eddy's effect on her life was to impose miraculous events. Norma started working as a typist in the radio script department of CBS and can recall clearly, even today, the events that followed.

> It was December 8, 1941, the day after the Japanese attacked Pearl Harbor and my job was frozen for the duration of the war. It proved to be most advantageous for me. I was able to meet celebrities

> like Jimmy Durante, Peter Lawford, Don DeFore, Ozzie and Harriet Nelson and of course Nelson Eddy.
>
> Not long after starting my job at CBS, my new friends asked me to join them for a visit to Nelson Eddy's show. They were going to ask him if he'd stop up and visit the script department after his rehearsal. We girls pulled it off so well that he happily obliged, but I had a singing lesson already scheduled and I explained to him that I would have to leave soon and would miss his visit. When he heard the words singing lesson, he started questioning me. After our conversation, I was so overwhelmed and intrigued by Nelson, I decided to ask my boss if he'd allow me to be the script girl for "The Electric Hour". I was so pesty and persistent, he reluctantly agreed.
>
> I became Nelson's script girl but I still wasn't satisfied. Usually a runner would deliver the typed scripts to the announcers, but I began quietly delivering the scripts myself. It worked for awhile until Nelson got suspicious and stopped to question me. I replied quite honestly, "I have great respect for you, and I love your music. I just want to help you and be your friend." I was wearing a navy blue dress with the initials NSN on it. Nelson asked what they stood for and I answered Norma Susanne Nelson. Not only was there the name association, but he seemed to like my honesty and directness. From that point on, I sat in on all rehearsals and met the guests he had on the show. I was referred to as "the special girl" of "The Electric Hour". In fact, I was written up in the fan club's publication, "The Shooting Star", as the show's mystery girl.

Nelson's reputation for helping young singers was well known and Norma was no exception. As long as she proved her trustworthiness and never exploited his friendship, Nelson would do anything he could to help her.

He personally auditioned her and made arrangements for her to study with Dr. Lippe for a few months.

> I used to visit the "G.E. House Party" in my spare time. One day, I told the pianist on the show that I was studying with Nelson Eddy's voice teacher and knew Nelson personally. The pianist doubted me, but he made me a very firm proposition. If I could get Nelson Eddy to appear on the "G.E. House Party", he would let me sing on a coast-to-coast hook-up.
>
> I immediately called Nelson and explained my dilemma and, without hesitation, he agreed to appear with me on "G.E. House Party". It was like a dream come true. Soon, all of CBS began rooting for me. My mother was in shock that an unknown little girl, such as myself, could get such a big chance. The fan magazine wrote, "Nelson Eddy and Robert Armbruster appoint themselves honorary godfathers to Norma Nelson."
>
> Nelson gave me something in life that no one else had ever given me: a belief in myself and the opportunity to use my talent. I have never known a more wonderful man and I am forever grateful to him. I continued to work as script girl for "The Electric Hour" while studying voice.
>
> My memories of those years with Nelson are still alive and vivid today. I remember Jeanette MacDonald's frequent visits to the "Electric Hour" and how Nelson and I used to rib each other. He was always a cut up---rehearsing in a favorite gray sweater that he wore so often, it eventually became thread bare.
>
> And, oh, how he loved a live audience! Ann would come down to the show as did Isabel; sometimes they even came together. He was relaxed and very much himself. Nelson once told me that he loved playing the part of the newspaper reporter in "Let Freedom

> Ring," because it brought back memories of his newspaper work. I remember how angry Nelson would become when people accused him of being in love with Jeanette. "Friends yes, lovers never," he would say.
>
> He had wanted to formally adopt Sidney but Ann felt it would be inappropriate. It was so evident to us how much he cared for Sid.
>
> He never complained about the guests with the exception of Oscar Levant. Oscar would come to rehearsal and inform Nelson that he really didn't have to practice because he was a genius. Nelson, being a practitioner of "practice makes perfect", could hardly adhere to that mentality!

Norma stayed on the show until 1946 and then moved to New York in order to further her career. Eventually, she married and retired from professional life to raise her family.

During all six years of "The Electric Hour", Bobby remembers Nelson being sick only once and that was when he had a bad cold. Bobby summed up Nelson's personality, "When he could be himself, he was alive, he was full of fun and relaxed---music was his life. But in pictures he always had to become someone else and he had a lot of regret about his motion picture image."

Mary Jo and Art Rush

The equestrian Nelson

Chicago Concert Series

HARRY ZELZER CONCERT MANAGEMENT

Presents

NELSON EDDY

BARITONE

THEODORE PAXSON, Pianist

CIVIC OPERA HOUSE ❖ CHICAGO

Monday Evening ❖ February 21 ❖ at 8:30 P.M.

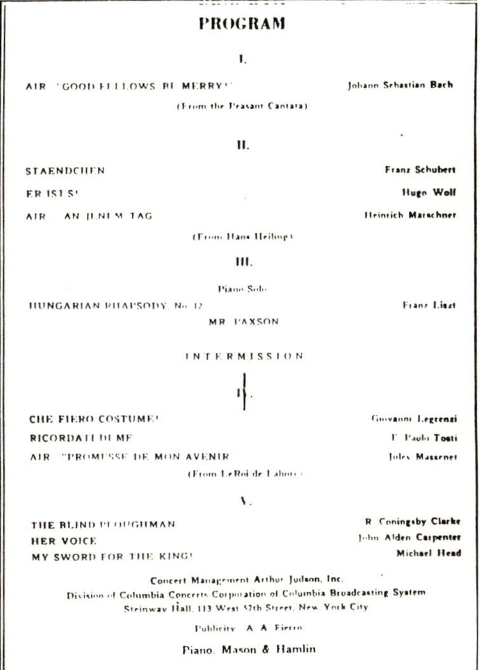

PROGRAM

I.

AIR "GOOD FELLOWS BE MERRY!" — Johann Sebastian **Bach**

(From the Peasant Cantata)

II.

STAENDCHEN — **Franz Schubert**

ER IST'S! — **Hugo Wolf**

AIR "AN JENEM TAG" — Heinrich **Marschner**

(From Hans Heiling)

III.

Piano Solo

HUNGARIAN RHAPSODY, No. 12 — Franz **Liszt**

MR. PAXSON

INTERMISSION

IV.

CHE FIERO COSTUME! — Giovanni **Legrenzi**

RICORDATI DI ME — F. Paolo **Tosti**

AIR "PROMESSE DE MON AVENIR" — Jules **Massenet**

(From Le Roi de Lahore)

V.

THE BLIND PLOUGHMAN — **R. Coningsby Clarke**

HER VOICE — John **Alden Carpenter**

MY SWORD FOR THE KING! — **Michael Head**

Concert Management Arthur Judson, Inc.

Division of Columbia Concerts Corporation of Columbia Broadcasting System

Steinway Hall, 113 West 57th Street, New York City

Publicity: A. A. Fierro

Piano, Mason & Hamlin

"New Moon"

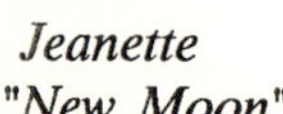

Jeanette
"New Moon"

Grauman's Chinese Theatre

"Chocolate Soldier" - Nelson, Nigel Bruce, Rise Stevens

"I Married An Angel"

"The Phantom of the Opera" - Nelson and Susanna Foster

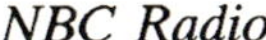

NBC Radio

Ronald Colman and Nelson

Frank Sinatra and Nelson

Benny Goodman and Nelson

Bob Hope, friend, Nelson

Adam & Eve

DoDo

DoDo

Singer Gets Temple Honor

Nelson Eddy is kissed by his wife after he receives honorary doctor of music degree at university's fourth annual music convocation. Robert L. Johnson, Temple president, made the presentation

Temple University

Teheran Hospital - 194

Complete Plans for War Fund Drive Meeting

At a meeting to be held Wednesday, March 15, in the Bruin theater, the local campaign for the American Red Cross War Fund will be opened. Pictured discussing plans for the affair are Mrs. Nelson Eddy of Brentwood, program chairman for the meeting, and Mrs. Janet Bullitt, West District director of the American Red Cross.

—Press Phot

Walt Disney and Nelson - "Make Mine Music"

Elsa Lanchester, Nelson, Ilona Massey - "Northwest Outpost"

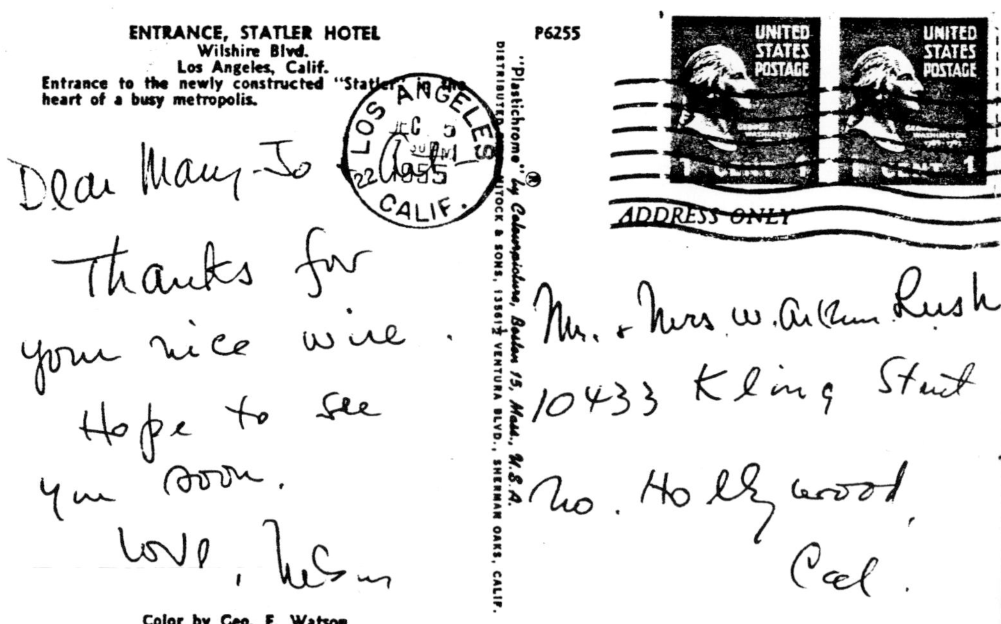

ENTRANCE, STATLER HOTEL
Wilshire Blvd.
Los Angeles, Calif.
Entrance to the newly constructed "Statler" in the heart of a busy metropolis.

P6255

"Plastichrome" by Colourpicture, Boston 15, Mass. U.S.A.
DISTRIBUTED BY ... TOCK & SONS, 13561½ VENTURA BLVD., SHERMAN OAKS, CALIF.

LOS ANGELES
DEC 5
1955
CALIF.

UNITED STATES POSTAGE
UNITED STATES POSTAGE

ADDRESS ONLY

Dear Mary-Jo & Al

Thanks for your nice wire. Hope to see you soon.

Love, Nelson

Mr. & Mrs. W. Allen Rush
10433 Kling Street
No. Hollywood,
Cal.

Color by Geo. E. Watson

Chapter Sixteen

Now that the weight of the turmoil and frustrations of his movie years was lifted from his shoulders, he continued doing what he loved best---concertizing. Concertizing was still a popular mode of entertainment in the early 40's. The war was producing a strange effect on Nelson's popularity. As he traveled the country, he noticed that instead of decreasing in size, his audiences were becoming larger than ever. In 1942, Nelson scheduled a 26 state concert tour. A survey in "Variety Magazine" revealed that Nelson Eddy and Lily Pons were the top earners in the field of concert performers, during that year. Normally, a top artist could earn approximately $42,000 a year. Nelson usually performed 25 to 30 concerts per year and received as high as $7,000 per concert. Generally $3,000 to $3,500 was the norm. Lily Pons averaged $3,000 and Jeanette MacDonald received $1,000 or over per engagement.

Nelson was now the top concert artist in the United States. His concerts, recordings and radio shows combined to bring him an average salary of $350,000 a year. After the government took its share and Nelson paid Ted, lawyers, household staff, accountants and business managers, he still made a remarkable salary for the early 40's.

As an artist and a showman, it was imperative that he coordinate his concert repertoire to the audiences needs and wishes. With the war in full swing, he was very careful to eliminate any sad or stressful songs from his concerts. He always started with the *Star Spangled Banner* and asked everyone to join in song with him. This brought about a closeness and camaraderie with the audience. He chose music to effect a release from the strain and consciousness of war. He avoided songs dealing with death, destruction and loss of love ones, and tried to select bright, yet not totally superficial, songs. He bowled them over town after town. Poised, well-tailored, handsomer than any baritone had a right to be, he held audience after audience to his side.

No other event in the Twentieth Century bonded the country closer together than the bombing of Pearl Harbor. The United States was now fully involved in the war and on the home front the country joined together to do their part. Nelson performed at many USO shows and worked long hours at the Hollywood Canteen. He was adamant that all vacant seats for his concerts be given to soldiers. At one scheduled concert in Des Moines, there were many cancellations due to poor weather conditions. He called Fort Des Moines Army Post and offered 150 soldiers the opportunity to attend his performance for free. Many of these young soldiers wrote him personal letters of thanks after attending his concert.

Ann always traveled with Nelson on the longer trips or she would fly in quietly to spend the weekends with him. She would sit in the wings of the theater and leave before or on the last encore. Whenever Ann was in the audience, Nelson's formal reserve loosened up with a myriad of hijinks. To the audience he appeared far more friendly than before, and in truth, he was. He would talk to almost anyone in sight whether he was in a restaurant, in the elevator, or on his way to his room because he knew Ann was waiting for him. This sudden change in his demeanor remained a paradox to many throughout the years, but those close to Nelson knew and understood the comfort that Ann brought to his hectic life. The three-day weekends were favorites because it gave them ample time to visit the museums and points of interest in each city. Later, it became increasing difficult for her to join him. The war was escalating at a faster pace and she had her ailing parents to care for at home.

The war was now shaping our history. Every day brought more disturbing news from overseas. America had gone patriotic and there were expectations on people, especially out on the West Coast. The bombing of Pearl Harbor had been too close for comfort and all efforts were being made by the population to secure the West Coast from the enemy. A strong feeling of fear and uneasiness existed. Fred MacMurray, Tryone Power, Gary Cooper and Nelson Eddy were air raid wardens in the Brentwood Heights area. This was very serious business indeed. They took courses on fire prevention, police routines, management of hand bombs, ditch digging and other duties.

There were 56 wardens in Nelson's district and if you lived in Brentwood, you could actually see the lights flash across the sky the minute a strange plane was heard overhead. It gave the residents a sense of security and comfort to know how alert the volunteers really were. The belief at the time, especially on the West Coast, was that women should stay home during the day and take care of the lighter warden duties. Ann was a daytime warden as were many other wives in Hollywood. She also worked tirelessly soliciting blood donations for the Red Cross Blood Bank. As everyone joined together to work for the cause of peace in Europe, the old Hollywood became a consolidated front of enthusiastic patriotism.

The Trocadero Restaurant had always been the most popular hangout for studio bosses, actors and directors in Hollywood. Everyone had busy schedules during the week, but on Saturday night, it was like a "family reunion". A real camaraderie existed among all involved in the studio system and Saturday night was a time to catch up on the gossip.

But the war was changing all that. Now the socializing was done at the Hollywood Canteen or the USO shows where together the actors, actresses, singers and dancers gathered to contribute their varied talents to the war effort.

Nelson often talked to his broadcast audience about his experiences as air raid warden. He described Fred MacMurray as "Senior Warden" in charge. One night he extolled Fred as a terror for discipline and punctuality, and went on to explain, "Tonight Fred's giving us incendiary bomb instructions and we'd better listen up or else". Fred loved Nelson's good natured patter and it helped to lighten the everyday burdens of the war on people's lives. When Nelson told of his adventures as an air raid warden, he bonded with the thousands of volunteer wardens across the country who were having similar experiences. (Fred MacMurray passed away in 1991.)

Through the broadcast and motion picture media, the country was becoming solidified in one shared effort and everyone understood very clearly who the enemy was. By 1942, the film studios were hard at work preparing their own versions of the fighting overseas. The hero's were American soldiers and the villains were the Germans and Japanese. There was no doubt about Hollywood's influence on the war effort; the contributions were numerous.

Nelson continued to make tour after tour performing at army hospitals and army camps throughout the United States. Before making "Phantom of the Opera" he signed a deal through J. Walter Thompson Agency to do the "Old Gold Radio Show." It debuted on CBS at 8:00, on Wednesday nights with Robert Armbruster once again conducting the orchestra. There was to be a mixed chorus of twelve voices. MGM had originally refused to release Nelson from his non-broadcasting provision in his studio contract, but later relented. Nelson signed the contract and agreed to work for $1.00 per broadcast if the firm distributed one million cigarettes weekly to the military personnel here and overseas. Please remember that in those days we were unaware of the effects that smoking had on our health. The deal drew popular approval at the time. With the approval of Secretary Morgenthau, and the Secretary of State in Washington, Nelson donated his salary each week to a different charity for the war effort and since he received $5,000 per broadcast and was slated to perform 52 weeks, he donated a total of $260,000 by the end of his contract.

There were many in his generation who might never have known good music had it not been for Nelson Eddy. He brought pleasure to thousands by his ability to sing both the light lyrical songs as well as difficult operatic arias. He had no criteria nor comparison with anyone else, for he was the only concert performer who performed lighter songs mixed with serious musical pieces. He was continuously enlarging his repertoire which he approximated to be 2000 songs. Throughout his career, no one could fault him on his diction and breath control which remain to this day a vocal standard for all singers. The quality of his tone was one of the most beautiful ever heard, but yet it was his kindliness towards the public and his gentle friendly personality which impassioned his fans. His magnetism came across the airways just as his intimacy had evolved when in the presence of his audiences. In films, in concert, over the radio or on records, the quality remained the same. It wasn't a trick of showmanship, it was his natural state of being.

Chapter Seventeen

Nelson's radio career now spanned 20 years and included appearances for "Newton Cole", "Dutch Masters", "General Motors", "Ford", "The Voice of Firestone", "Vicks", "Screen Guild", "Chase and Sanborn", "Family Theatre", "Lux Radio Theater", "Old Gold", his own show "The Electric Hour", "Bell Telephone Hour" and "Kraft Music Hall".

He had a tremendous number of fine artists working with him on the air during these fabulous radio years. The list is too long to name everyone, but of those recorded are: Benny Goodman, Frank Sinatra, Victor Borge, Rise Stevens, Jo Stafford, Jeanette MacDonald, Dorothy Kirsten, Dorothy Lamour, Don Ameche, Rudy Vallee, Oscar Levant, Dinah Shore, Rosalind Russell, Ginny Simms, Red Skelton, Shirley Temple, Ronald Coleman, W.C. Fields, Clark Gable, Marilyn Monroe, Hoagy Carmichael, Kathryn Grayson, Jane Powell, Eleanor Steber, Nadine Connor, Francia White, Margaret Speaks and Lois Butler.

Nelson, Ted and Dr. Lippe spent as much time together as they could. It was hard to believe that so many years had passed since their first meeting. Although Dr. Lippe's health had begun to fail, nothing could stop him from working with Nelson whenever time allowed.

Ted and Nelson would regale Lippe with their experiences on the road. Ted never missed a concert tour. He was always there to accompany Nelson while instilling his own style and talent into the program. Ted played the versatile music of Chopin or Beethoven so eloquently that the audience would applaud for more.

Ted loved to do the encores. No matter what he chose to play, he was a pianist who performed with talent, fire and sensitivity. As Nelson and Ted traveled the United States, Helen Paxson and Ann Eddy were united in their loyalty and support. In the early years, Helen was even more homebound than Ann because she and Ted had two young sons to raise. As the boys grew older, she was able to join Ann on the long weekend trips. Their friendship was one of trust and understanding.

Nelson and Ted had been together for so long that they took each other for granted. Every once in awhile, Nelson would liven things up by pulling one of his humorous hijinks on Ted. After so many successes, Nelson nicknamed Ted "the perfect victim". Most of the time Ted caught on to Nelson's pranks but had difficulty in determining exactly when Nelson would strike. Ted was by nature a rather quiet, subdued person. He was also a procrastinator and Nelson always chided him about getting things done.

A typical example is the episode of Ted's suitcases. Ted had been dragging around the same suitcases for years. They were ripped and torn in many places. Nelson never missed an opportunity to badger Ted about their appearance. One day, while they were standing on the station platform awaiting the arrival of their train, Nelson began to kick Ted's suitcases about. Since he had been ribbing Ted about his tattered suitcases for months, Ted decided to ignore him. It was bad enough that Nelson always replaced his own suitcases as soon as they began to show the least amount of wear.

"What a relic", Nelson teased, as he kicked Ted's case. "Aren't you afraid someone will steal it?" Then Nelson began to jump up and down on Ted's suitcase causing Ted to react. "Hey, knock it off Nelson, that's all I've got", he pleaded. Nelson simply ignored Ted and continued to jump up and down while smiling gleefully. The madder Ted got, the harder Nelson jumped, until finally, his six-foot-two inch frame managed to break the suitcase wide apart. What a sight! Just when Nelson felt that Ted had really had it, a co-conspirator walked up to Ted carrying a beautiful set of new fitted suitcases. Nelson had had them especially made for Ted as a birthday gift. Ted's face spoke a thousand words!

George Brown was another victim of Nelson's practical jokes. As his concert manager and close friend, George traveled with Nelson and Ted and was an integral part of the trio until his early death. Nelson used to tell George that he hated surprises, but that by no means included Nelson pulling them off on somebody else. George needed a good laugh now and then because he had the difficult task of handling the problems that arose on the concert tours. George's greatest concern was for Nelson's safety and with thousands of fans enthralled by him it was not an easy job. Nelson kept a private list of fans who he felt might be potential problems. Any person in the public eye is constantly on the alert for those fans which show erratic or fanatical behavior. Year after year, Nelson's popularity increased the demand for tighter security. For protection George ushered Nelson out of the side door of the theater or he would place policemen on the running board of his car. At the hotels, there were guards stationed at his door, but Nelson never questioned George's decisions, especially after one very disquieting experience.

Nelson had recently received life threatening notes and George immediately contacted the FBI. After a brief investigation, the FBI substantiated that the notes were the "real McCoy". Much to his dismay, the security around him was increased even more. As Nelson later explained:

> I couldn't tell the truth to the press because it would interfere with the police investigation. It makes

> you feel kind of funny when you get notes saying, if you don't leave $50,000 in a certain place, a member of a gang in Hollywood will kill your mother. During the investigation, I was already a bit uneasy, when one day, out of nowhere, a guy grabbed me and said, "Are you Mr. Eddy?" My heart sank down to my feet and I thought well, this is it, but thank goodness, he turned out to be a railroad representative. By the way, I have never liked that fellow ever since.

When the case was finally solved, Nelson applauded George for all his help. "George added a lot of grey hairs to his head on my behalf", chided Nelson.

As the years passed, Nelson's philosophy of life became more developed. An overview of his philosophy would describe him to be a "seeker of truth". No matter from whom it came or how many times he had to lay aside preconceived opinions---his desire was to search out truth. He used the word truth so very gracefully. I believe he meant that he wanted to be in harmony with his universe, his God and all others, as much as it was humanly possible.

An insatiable student, he loved to read theology, philosophy and biographies. His favorite philosopher was Will Durant. In many ways he shared Durant's philosophy of life. His religious and moral philosophy extended into everything he did. One of his greatest joys was to converse with others about their ideals and philosophies.

He was a firm believer in today's "new age" philosophy. Far before his time, he theorized that everyone is empowered to change his or her own life. He believed each person is responsible for where they are in the scheme of things. As Nelson described it, "Take a glance at your present status and it will reveal what you have desired most. No one is really cheated, for the responsibility falls upon you and I. I can't believe that God would go to all the trouble of creating us and providing unlimited blessings for our pleasure and comfort only that we might learn to make a little money and spend it all on ourselves."

Sidney remembers that Nelson had a habit of constantly reevaluating his motives---he developed a check list to make sure he was on track. As a purist, with a strong value system, it was imperative to Nelson that he understand his own motives. Nelson saw himself as a failure in the little things in life; he was impatient and very short tempered. He often told the story about how he had mistreated his chauffeur. Shortly after stardom had laid claim to him, Nelson was feeling high and mighty. One day he bawled out the chauffeur just because the poor man wasn't paying attention and made a wrong turn. The next day, a guilt-ridden Nelson discovered that the chauffeur's mother had died the day before. Quick to acknowledge his shortcomings, he usually berated himself while promising to improve.

His personal habits mirrored his philosophy in life. Around home, he loved to wear old clothes and work in the yard. He always took great pride in his surroundings and loved to spend time in his home. While rehearsing his radio show, he clung to the old rehearsal jacket that he cherished. When someone presented him with a new jacket, he wore it twice and fluffed his lines. The next day he got rid of it and went back to his old jacket because he believed it brought him luck. Yet he never wore his dress suits for long periods of time. For years, he had been sending them off to his father. They wore the same size in suits and shoes and although Bill was one half inch taller than Nelson, their clothes fit each other like a glove. Throughout the years, Ann faithfully sent off the suits and Bill proudly wore each and every one of them.

In appointments, Nelson was always very prompt, and he would become very impatient with anyone who didn't value the same promptness he did. When appearing in public, he was known for his meticulous dress which was always color coordinated. He was not a glamour boy in the normal sense of the word, just very well put together. Serious minded by nature, he was remarkably spontaneous in temperament. He was known to be extremely congenial and down to earth in live conversation and was gifted in the art of light-hearted bantering.

Chapter Eighteen

As 1942 drew to a close, Nelson looked with pride upon all he had accomplished. He had triumphed in every area of show business he had ever tried; be it opera, the concert stage, movies, records or radio. Nelson was his music---from German Lieder to *"Shortnin' Bread"*, he had become the complete vocal master. If anyone would have told him how drastically his career would change in later life, no one would have believed it, least of all the gentle troubadour, Nelson Eddy.

Sidney was in the army now and found it difficult to get home on leave. He had joined thousands of America's young sons and daughters in the fight for freedom over tyranny. Being away from home and family was lonely and depressing. Families suffered too as they tried to find ways to share their time honored traditions with their loved ones far away. Nothing brought these feelings home as strongly as the Christmas holidays.

Ann was a master in the art of gift giving. Her preparations for Christmas were famous. About mid-October she would set up a card table in the master bedroom and carefully make a list of gifts to buy for everyone. Then she would lovingly search for each gift. Her talent for gift wrapping was truly an art. She would personally wrap each gift with a multitude of velvet, satin and lace bows. The gifts were beautiful to look at---let alone open. Nelson and Ann had special holiday traditions that were followed faithfully year after year. Each year, the Eddys would exchange an elegantly decorated Christmas ornament with Jeanette and Gene. Each family was allowed to keep the ornament for only one season and the next

Christmas, it would be exchanged again. The Paxsons also shared a similar tradition with the Eddy's; they exchanged a beautiful bronze statue every year. These yearly exchanges continued until their respective deaths.

Although Sidney was far away, he was not forgotten as a multitude of Ann's beautifully wrapped gifts arrived to brighten his Christmas. Ann and Nelson would gift their dear friends Art and Mary Jo Rush and Wayne and Elinor Griffin with the cleverest of items. They were always very meaningful gifts; money was not the object.

One year, the entire Rush family received a donation to a new clinic of the Children's Hospital in Los Angeles in their name. Nelson wrote in his letter to the Rushs:

> Instead of buying, wrapping and sending you a gift, we have made a donation in your name. It is as though you yourselves were giving a helping hand to a crippled child at this Christmas-time. We hope that the slight disappointment of not "gettin' sump'n" will be replaced by the satisfaction that a practical human need is being met. With heartfelt Holiday Greetings and kindest good wishes for the coming year. We are ---lovingly yours, Ann and Nelson.

He also enclosed a picture of the handicapped child their donation would benefit. Virginia Eddy was not to be out done.

> I never knew what to give Nelson for Christmas because he had everything. In 1942, I spent my freshman year at Colby College in Waterville, Maine so I decided to give him a real down home gift. I selected twelve very perfect Maine potatoes, wrapped each individually in Christmas paper and sent them off to him. The response was great!

Nelson's love of art led to an avid interest in pewter. After visiting hundreds of art galleries and museums, he began to amass pieces of pewter from private collectors. This sudden obsession seemed to overtake his normal level-headed sense of balance. Sidney recalls that the music room was turned into one large pewter store. After purchasing several total collections, Nelson realized he had not been selective in his choices. He returned the house to order by giving away most of the collection, keeping only a few choice pieces.

He studied the seventeenth century English painters and turned his concentration to carefully building a small but unique collection. He eventually added modern French paintings to the collection. As an artist, he believed that painting was unspoken poetry and the artist was communicating his dreams. His art collection was considered one of outstanding quality by many art dealers and collectors. Eventually, he added some of his own paintings to the collection.

Although their contracts with MGM were finished, Nelson and Jeanette were always receptive to the various opportunities that might provide a reunion for them. Universal Studios had wanted to pair them in the remake of the operetta "East Wind", but the studio lost interest. MGM purchased "The Vagabond King" from Paramount for Nelson and Jeanette, but the project never came to fruition. "The Vagabond King" was finally remade in 1956 starring Kathryn Grayson and Oreste. MGM also bought the screen rights of "Show Boat" for a remake with Nelson and Jeanette, but again the project never materialized. It wasn't until 1951 that Kathryn Grayson and Howard Keel filmed a color version of "Show Boat" for MGM.

In 1943, Universal offered Nelson the romantic lead in the remake of "The Phantom of the Opera". He loved the part so much after reading the script, that he even agreed to wear a wig and mustache. Although no one ever quite understood why he had to change his appearance, Nelson felt it was a small price to pay for such a wonderful opportunity. And in truth, it proved to be a rewarding experience for him. He later included the music from "Phantom" in his concert repertoire.

Susanna Foster had the female lead in "Phantom of the Opera". She emerged as a beautiful starlet in her film debut. She was only 18 years old when she signed a term contract, but Nelson felt she had star quality. When interviewed, he commented, "Susanna's a coming sensation, mark my words. She's an adult young lady, poised with perfect aplomb and she can hit above high 'C' which, if I know my soprano lingo, is just about in Ripley's class."

Susanna met Nelson before they ever made "Phantom" together. In remembering him, she spoke in very respectful terms.

> I was eighteen when I attended a party at W. S. Van Dyke's house. At the time, my singing teacher was teaching Woody Van Dyke's wife to sing. Charles Spears was a publicity agent and he told me Universal was seeking a female lead for "Phantom of the Opera" because Diana Durbin didn't want to do it. I came to the party to be interviewed and auditioned. Nelson was also at the party and he introduced himself to me and we talked for a long while. He was the most harmonious man I have ever met.
>
> I was very young and naive at the time, but I knew what other young actresses had experienced while making a movie. I'd heard stories about many of the stars who were not moral nor gentle. On those movie sets, respect was non-existent. But on the set of "Phantom of the Opera" there was no vulgarity because it was not permitted in Nelson's presence. That was

unheard of behavior! He simply enhanced the quality of all those around him.

There was a lot of fun on the set. Fritz Feld would play old German and Viennese songs on the piano and Nelson and I would entertain in between our takes. It was a wonderful experience. My most lasting memory of Nelson was when he walked into my dressing room one day while I was being prepared for one of the takes and he sat down quietly and took my hands in his. He said, "Susanna, I am 42 years of age and you are young, vibrant and just beginning a wonderful career. What a wonderful life is in front of you. I want to wish you the very best." I shall never forget that moment, it meant so much to me.

I remember that Nelson gave the cast and cameramen exquisite leather bound books. It was his way to choose something for everyone that came straight from his heart. He was a very sensitive man. He gave me a beautifully inscribed copy of "Indian Love Lyric". Hal Mohr, one of our photographers was a rough and tough guy, but intellectually bright and Nelson gave him a collection of "Aristophanes". Hal was so deeply touched.

Hindsight is so much clearer than foresight. After making "Phantom of the Opera", Nelson offered me the opportunity to go on concert tour with him, but I was too young and too scared, and I didn't know the languages. Concertizing was "big time". Now in retrospect, I know that Nelson would have protected and guided me as he did so many others. I will carry that regret for the rest of my life.

When I met Jeanette MacDonald for the first time, it was during the filming of the "Firefly". We had the same attorney and I was invited to a dinner party at Jeanette's home for just the four of us. Jeanette was a very charming and down to earth person and her happiness with Gene was strongly in evidence. I was well aware of the rumors and libelous statements often

> made about Nelson and Jeanette, but I knew none of it was true. I knew them both as honorable and ethical people. Everyone who knew them knows this to be true. There will always be those who thrive on imagination and made-up stories to fit their own needs. Someone once told me that Jeanette looked pregnant in one scene in "Sweethearts" where Nelson and Jeanette sing "Pretty As A Picture" and they chose to assume it was with Nelson's child. What rubbish---it's sick and it's sad, and it proves to me that they can do anything to you when your dead and unable to defend yourself.

Nelson concentrated on his concerts as the film scripts were less and less desirable to him. In 1944, he appeared to a sold out crowd at a concert in Carnegie Hall. That evening, Dad Eddy, as he was often called, and the whole family were seated in the front row. Bill always referred to his son as "the boy" and how proud he was of his boy, Nelson. The fan clubs remember that Dad Eddy and Isabel were always involved in Nelson's life. Thelma Cohen, a dear friend and President of Nelson's fan club for many years, believed that Nelson had inherited his sense of humor from his father because she remembers, "That man could spin a yarn like nobody else". Bill and Marguerite would often join the fan club members for lunch.

Nelson's radio shows continued to do well and his sponsors were elated. Guest appearances included such stars as Shirley Temple, Kathryn Grayson, and of course, Jeanette MacDonald. Shirley Temple made her radio debut on Nelson's "Electric Hour".

But there is one guest star that shines above all the others. Nelson was fantastically proud of his mother and as Thelma Cohen recalls, "It was a Mother's Day broadcast where Nelson asked Isabel to sing with him a song she'd taught him long ago, *Love's Old Sweet Song.* After they had finished a lilting version of the song, Nelson exclaimed with unconcealed pride, 'Yes sir, that's my mommy'. The live audience went wild."

Nelson still found several movie scripts appealing and when he realized that the script of "Knickerbocker Holiday" had a minor role for a freedom loving newspaper publisher in the 1600's, he couldn't resist. Besides, he had wisely invested money in the original Broadway production of "Knickerbocker Holiday" starring Walter Houston and he held the production rights for the film version. It was the perfect opportunity to produce as well as act. The movie starred Charles Coburn who played the main character and sang the memorable *September Song.* Constance Dowling starred with him. Unfortunately, Nelson chose to cast himself in the least advantageous role. Although his priority in agreeing to do the movie was admirable, the timing was all wrong. With the world at war, audiences were not interested in fantasy. The movie did poorly at the box office.

Chapter Nineteen

During these difficult years, Nelson continued to entertain the troops. The USO tours were his favorite shows. The soldiers wanted the stars to be themselves and they let certain stars know when they were phoney. Nelson was totally without pretense and they loved him for it. Nelson and Ted traveled without fanfare or publicity to the remotest of stations to entertain the troops. Christmas of 1944 holds the most vivid memories of these trips. Two old friends of Nelson's from Columbia Concerts actually arranged the USO shows for him. His assignment---Africa. Smallpox, cholera, typhoid and typhus shots were a small price to pay in the name of freedom. Whatever their natural reluctance at being away from home on Christmas, any star who traveled the USO circuits will tell you, it was more than compensated for by the joys of bringing happiness to our boys overseas. Danger was of little consequence, in fact, the hardships were exhilarating. It proved to the soldiers we were all for one and one for all.

They flew first to Puerto Rico and then to British Guiana and over the Brazilian jungles to Belem where, in a large hanger, everyone stood up in the heat and humidity while Nelson and Ted did a concert. It was a rousing success. Then on to the Ascension Islands, where they gave four outdoor concerts.

The next day they flew into Accra on the Gold Coast of Africa. In fifty-one working days they covered 35,000 miles and had given fifty-six concerts in addition to visiting the hospitals, mess halls and officer's clubs. They played to an audience of 300 in a hospital ward and to 6,000 sitting out on the ground in an airfield. As Nelson would later state, "These soldiers wanted the best music. The most frequent requests were *The Lord's Prayer* and *Ave Maria*.

Pianos appeared as if by magic and an organ was flown into Chartoum and stayed with them throughout the journey. They met and performed for the King of Egypt; he even raided the ice box with them one night.

They performed for the American, British, Persian and Russian legations. They sang to railroad men, truckers, longshoremen, anyone who happened to be around at the time they were performing. And after all of this, they came nearest to disaster on the trip home. They hit stormy weather over the Azores while they were 17,000 feet up; they had very little oxygen and no radio. But somehow, after all their travels, they took the whole thing very calmly. After landing, the pilot explained how lucky they were to have escaped disaster.

While Nelson was entertaining the troops, doing warden duty and singing the command performance broadcasts, another ugly rumor reared its head. Only this time it originated from Manchester, England. No one had a stronger belief in America and its traditions than Nelson Eddy. That made him the perfect target for the German propaganda machine which tried to discredit him by announcing he had joined the German Air Force. It may sound ludicrous to us today, but during those difficult frightening times, rumors could easily be perceived as truths to be feared. Fortunately for Nelson, Ben Lyon of the BBC adamantly denied the rumor with solid facts. Nelson Eddy, a hero to millions, had been just another target. Many stars suffered similar attempts by the German propaganda efforts to discredit their honor, but to no avail.

After the war, Sidney Jr. headed back to college at the Missouri School of Mines and Metals where he studied Electrical Engineering. In 1945, Nelson performed in a memorial concert to Jerome Kern. He also did bond drive performances with Jack Benny, Alan Ladd, Ester Williams, Jo Stafford and Lionel Barrymore while continuing his radio appearances on the "Hollywood Victory Show", "Mail Call", and "Here's to the Veterans" .

When Walt Disney asked Nelson to become the voice of Willie the Whale in "Make Mine Music", Nelson was so excited about the opportunity he couldn't stop talking about it. For fifteen years, he had been recording his voice over and over again on his recording machine and was able to blend various pitches by playing one voice over the other. He had created a method of recording that had never been done on film before. He actually invented the multiple recording process to produce the chorus affect. Walt knew of Nelson's success with his recording machine---it was time to get together and discuss the project.

As Nelson recalled:

> I visited Disney's office and read the story of Willie. Disney said it was a good story but could never be done. I asked, "Do you mind if I take it home?" I wrote the whole thing and planned it and then presented it to Disney. It was better than what came on the screen. I had something from Hansel and Gretel---more opera. When I finished, Disney said nothing. I thought I was sunk. Then he pressed a button and about six men came flying in.

Ted added, "From all over, the walls, the desk, etc. They agreed to do it, just like you see in the movies."

"Make Mine Music" was filmed at RKO Studios and released in 1946. Nelson loved every minute of being Willie the Whale. He had the good company of Benny Goodman, Dinah Shore, The Andrew Sisters and Jerry Colonna. During the filming of "Make Mine Music", Nelson took the entire cast and crew of "The Electric Hour" over to Disney Studios for his radio broadcasts.

There is a twelve minute sequence where he does "The Whale Who Wanted to Sing at the Met", narrating and singing every role from bass to soprano. The climax is Nelson singing with himself chorus style. It was an outstanding creation of both voice and recording know-how, but the critics were less kind. It was perceived as being not quite up to Disney's usual standards. Today it is considered a classic.

When the war years ended, America settled down to a more relaxed and upbeat style of living. Families began to purchase tracks of land in the outskirts of towns and cities. Nelson was still on the concert tour, but even he was beginning to feel the affect of the shifting economic patterns as Americans settled into new life styles. More important, there were new electronic devices on the horizon. Television had been invented in the 1930's, but broadcasting had been suspended until after the war. Now television stations began to sprout up all across the country. America was spellbound by this visual magic created right in their own living rooms.

No doubt about it, things were changing. Nelson and Ann found more free time to get away, even if only for short trips. Sometimes they took five day car trips up the California coast or to the Oregon coast. They loved to sneak away to go fishing. Nelson was happy to be home. He loved to put on his old clothes and work in the back yard. This had become his favorite form of exercise.

He agreed to make one more movie with his beloved friend Ilona Massey for Republic Pictures in 1947. Elsa Lanchester, Joseph Schildkraut and Hugo Hass joined them. The script was very cleverly written for a romantic melodrama. This time Nelson wanted an outstanding musical effort. As Nelson tells it, he was lured into doing "Northwest Outpost" because he was told the musical score was by Rudolf Friml. Friml had written the successful score for "Rose Marie" and Nelson believed it would be a quality product.

After signing the contract, Nelson went over to Friml's house to hear the music only to discover that there wasn't any music. Not one note had been composed! Of course, Friml offered to compose anything Nelson wanted, but time was of the essence. The final musical score was quickly compiled and of the utmost disappointment to Nelson.

Oddly enough, the critics and the audiences liked the movie. The Los Angeles Times even claimed that "Northwest Outpost" restored Nelson to the screen. The film was shown in Europe under its original title "End of the Rainbow" and made a good box office play. It was an upbeat ending to Nelson's movie career. He wanted no more promises and no more painful disappointments.

In all the years that Nelson starred in films, the studios had never pushed him to take serious acting lessons. In fact, the studio frowned on such activity because they felt he was so natural in his innocence and naivete that they didn't want to tamper with the ingredients. It was a major part of his charm because he was so honest about his awkwardness. Later, Alexander Smallens was to recall that acting was definitely not his strong point, but that in "straight roles" his singing and warm manner conquered any audience. In fact, any part with broad comedy also perfectly suited Nelson's own sense of fun and those were the parts he loved to play.

From the beginning, the very issue that influenced his decision to make movies had nothing to do with success. He never really believed that stardom would be his, and if he had known the trials and tribulations that the public would place upon him, would he have chosen otherwise?

But Nelson never looked back. Like a martinet, he would continue to work because he believed he had to work. He would find a different arena to perform in.

Chapter Twenty

In 1947 the Nelson Eddy Fan Club won a cup for being the most successful fan club of its kind. Nelson loved his fans and when his club won the award, he came to personally thank them. Many of the members recall Nelson standing before them beaming with pride. He endeared himself to them in so many ways. He never kept himself aloof from those he came to know and recognize over the years, and there are countless instances where he went out of his way to show them kindness and consideration. Many of his original fan club members are alive and well today, still loyal to this gracious and endearing man. New fan clubs, though smaller in size, still gather today to remember both Nelson and Jeanette.

All was calm in the Eddy household when Louella Parsons wrote in her column "Nelson is going to be a grandfather". How could this be? Sidney wasn't even married. Ann was livid! She called Louella immediately and asked her to retract the statement. The next time Louella's column appeared---she wrote "Oops, they aren't even married." Ann took any form of impropriety very seriously and she never forgave Louella for "dirtying" the family name. Sidney's wedding to Mary Alice Sheffield-Cassan took place two months later on March 6, 1947, but there were no grandchildren until several years later. In fairness to Louella, it was the one and only time she ever gave out mis-information about the Eddys and Nelson would always remain grateful to her for that. Sidney and Mary Alice moved to Malibu. But instead of using his college degree in engineering, Sidney followed his fathers footsteps and went to work at MGM's production department. He was a natural.

There were celebrations on the Eddy side too, but they were mixed with great disappointment. Virginia was graduating from Rhode Island State College (University of Rhode Island) in June and the college wanted to give Nelson an honorary degree during the commencement. It was to be a double celebration, but he was unable to attend because of his concert schedule. Ginny was saddened but Bill was broken hearted.

At Jeanette and Gene's 12th wedding anniversary, Nelson laughed as he lifted up his glass to toast, "I think I'm the one to propose this toast. After all, I've married her more often than you have." Would there ever be a film to reunite Nelson and Jeanette? They received many such offers, but they were committed to wait for the perfect vehicle for their talents. Unfortunately, they were presented with so many "Grade B" opportunities and, rather than submit to another failure, they agreed to leave on a high note. Nelson and Jeanette continued to appear together on radio programs such as "Lux Radio Theatre", "Screen Guild Theatre" and "Kraft Music Hall". Ann, Jeanette, Gene and Nelson often reminisced about their movies and the wonderful times they shared in making them.

The world was being rocked by a new fear---Communism. Hollywood, having been one of the most dedicated fronts in supporting the fight for freedom, was now a target of the House Committee on Un-American Activities. The town was rocked with turmoil as actors and writers were black listed. It divided every creative effort and ruined friendships forever. Nelson was deeply affected by this terrible scene as many of his old friends were involved. Yet he was quietly relieved to be away from the travesty.

By 1948 Milton Berle had soared to popularity by capturing a national television audience. The impact of television was monumental and the movie studios began to suffer. Then, in 1948, anti-trust laws went into effect, and the U.S. Supreme Court added to the studios' woes by requiring them to relinquish much of their control. Film attendance declined drastically and independent producers began to rebel against the studios. By 1949, television had captured the hearts of America. Americans were buying 100,000 television sets a week. Louis B. Mayer was still head of MGM, but he was losing ground very fast. As the film studios crumbled, many of Nelson's peers were forced to retire because they could not make the transition from movies to television. With his star status safely in the hands of loyal and numerous fans, it was a time for Nelson to reflect on all that was happening around him.

Nelson turned down the starring role in "South Pacific" because there wasn't enough singing in the part. The role later went to Enzio Pinza. He continued to perform in concerts across the country.

Dad Eddy was to be disappointed once again when Nelson's concert commitments kept him from singing at Ginny's wedding to John Lloyd Brown on April 21, 1949 in Pawtucket, Rhode Island. Nelson hated the constant disappointment he caused his family. Just once, it would have been wonderful to have been there in person.

He performed to a sold out audience of 22,000 on Easter as well as to a packed audience at a Christmas benefit for tuberculosis. After suffering the hardships of being on the road for so long, he needed to carry a lighter load for awhile. His back had gone out several times and the pain and immobility caused him to slow down. While Ann worked in civic affairs and did volunteer work for the Community Chest, Nelson pursued his art work and many hobbies. He added tap dancing and gymnastics to strengthen his back and maintain his physical condition.

By 1949, the song *Shortnin' Bread* was at its height. Nelson received two thousand recipes for "shortnin' bread" and finally created his own recipe. Thousands of people were now eating "shortnin' bread". When he made his 20th concert tour, Louella Parsons wrote, "That boy goes on forever; he is so popular. I get letters, letters, letters." Ann was still not speaking to Louella. Nelson's critics were giving him rave reviews, albeit a bit more reserved. Nelson appeared in concert at Keil Auditorium and the St. Louis Star Times wrote: "The name Nelson Eddy doesn't quite convey the glamor it used to whenever radio and movie enthusiasts congregated a decade ago. But he has plenty of the magnetism left for concert-goers and he still captivates an audience. His hair is platinum under the spot lights and he generates the same charisma."

The radio shows continued to do very well. Dorothy Kirsten of the Metropolitan Opera co-starred with Nelson on the summer version of Kraft Music Hall and it was an instantaneous success. Bobby Armbruster joined Nelson on Kraft Music Hall and the two of them had a great time playing off each others' well-developed senses of humor. In fact, one night Bobby surprised the audience by revealing a singing voice shockingly similar to that of Dennis Day. It was a happy time in the Eddy's life, but it was not to last.

This time it was Isabel who stirred the calm waters. She had no intention of growing old gracefully and was easily bored and often cantankerous. She would call Ann and Nelson on numerous occasions to announce that she needed a change of scenery. To Isabel, a change of scenery meant a complete move, but to Nelson, it meant a trip. After much persuasion, Isabel always heeded Nelson's advice. She would disappear for a month and return home perfectly content until the next time. He'd tease her saying the Eddy's have "vagabond blood in their genes". Nelson loved his mother completely and would provide anything for her comfort and well-being.

He also needed to take care of his own pressing concerns. He was very cognizant of the realities facing him at this stage of his life. For all practical purposes, his movie career was over and he realized that the concert tours would also diminish in time. The studio's had sought out new talent to capture the audience of the Post War era and many of the older actors and actresses of the 30's were fading into oblivion.

Everyone perceived Nelson to be a very wealthy man, but in reality he wasn't. In fact, most of the stars of that era were not. They did not have the royalties from re-runs and other legal protection that exist for the stars of today. The fight over residuals had not yet begun and the older stars would never reclaim the money that should have been rightfully theirs. They either chose to spend their money as they earned it or save for the future.

Ever cautious, Nelson and Ann agreed that it was time to scale down. The house was very expensive to keep up and it had been almost impossible to find the needed help during the war. Now the cost of hiring a grounds keeper and staff had nearly tripled. They put the house on the market for $95,000.00

June Haver recalls how she discovered Nelson's house again after many years:

> After my marriage to Fred MacMurray, we began the chore of house hunting. After several months of utter frustration, we came to the conclusion that Beverly Hills was inappropriate for our midwestern tastes. It had to feel like home to us and so far we had come up empty handed. Then one day, our

realtor called and asked if I would like to look at a vacant home in Brentwood. His description had piqued my interests. But when I pulled up in front of the house, I was even more entranced by its design because it looked like "home". As we entered the foyer, I was overwhelmed with a feeling of "knowing". It was then that the realtor explained that we were standing in the prized home of Nelson Eddy. The realtor had been an air raid warden with Nelson during the war, and although he admired Nelson's home, he had never had the opportunity to see the inside, so he was as excited as I was. I immediately fell in love with the house and the lasting impression of my earlier visit to Nelson's home came rushing back to me. Fred and I bought that house the very next day.

We've lived here for thirty-six years now and our daughters have asked that we never sell it. I feel sure it will be passed down through our family for years to come.

Nelson didn't miss a trick. Even the outside of the house is landscaped perfectly with the correct trees and southern magnolias. So the home looks like a true "Williamsburg home".

Several years after we moved in, Fred suggested we lower the ceiling in the domed music room because he thought it would make the room a little cozier. I wasn't real sure about this decision, but agreed to go along with it. But the best part is what we discovered in the music room. While reconstructing the ceiling, the workman had to remove six square panels around the fireplace in order to put in the fake ceiling, and that's when we found this strange hole in the wall. I would call it a "peep hole". When you looked into the hole, there was a carved out space and all we could see was a light bulb dangling from a wire. We were all totally perplexed; what in the world could this be? Fred's curiosity got the best of him and he called Nelson. Nelson and Gale Sherwood were doing their

> night club act in San Francisco at that time and Nelson invited us for a visit. He got such a kick out of Fred's "third degree". We were all anxious to see each other. It wasn't two minutes after we went back stage before Fred zeroed in on the mystery. Fred said, "Okay, Nelson, let's have it---what in the world did you have behind that wall?"
>
> Nelson burst out laughing and said, "Well, I had my favorite toy, a top, that I had cherished from my childhood. It was quite a conversation piece. I would flip on the switch and look into the peep hole and there was my beautiful multicolored top in its own private little show place." What a wonderful whimsy that man possessed. We found so many special additions that Nelson had added to his home.

Fred and June cherish their home and it is as warm and welcoming today as it was thirty-eight years ago.

The Eddy's wanted a house which they could care for themselves, but they also wanted to be near their dear friends Elinor and Wayne Griffin. They found a shaded spanish style home located directly across the street from the Griffins at 155 South Hudson in Hancock Park. It was the perfect choice. Elinor has many fond memories of the years they spent together as neighbors. A book about Elinor's life and music was recently written by Virginia Bortin. In it she reminisces about family and friends. She remembers her children playing baseball in the street with Nelson and Wayne.

> There was hardly any traffic and the children called Nelson, "Uncle Nelson". They loved the ball games and all the children in the neighborhood would join in. In the evening we would go to each others homes for dinner. There was always music after dinner. I would pull out a book of Brahms and ask Nelson if he was

> interested in singing. Then Wayne and Ann would sit quietly on the sofa and never speak a word while I played and Nelson sang song after song. He would often sing an entire book of compositions.

Elinor described Nelson as an "innately beautiful musician with an exceptionally beautiful voice." She felt he often underrated himself and that inside he was a very shy person. Elinor remembers how Ann was alone a great deal of the time, but in every conversation she always used the shared terminology "we". "We" decided to do this or "we" decided to do that. Elinor was impressed by the fact that Ann and Nelson talked over every decision that was made regarding his career and their lives together. If he was on the road, they would talk at least twice a day. Elinor explained:

> Ann was a very strong woman; she learned very early that she had to deal with a husband in the limelight. Ann was the most loyal kind of person. Anybody who has a husband in the public eye becomes very philosophical. Ann understood every facet of her role and she accepted it with grace and style. Ann often told me how much she cherished the quiet years that she and Nelson spent together out of the limelight, but she knew it wouldn't last.
>
> One time he bought a new tie and was showing it off. He loved to shop and always made a point of shopping in the neighborhood, because he believed it helped support the community. He loved to be in his home. He took great pride in his flowers, shrubs and garden. He loved being a neighbor and was like a little child about it, so excited to share and help whenever he could. During this time he spent a great deal of time on his art work.
>
> Nelson was very seldom upset. In fact, most of the time, I recall him as being happy. And that is how most of his friends remember him---"a very happy soul".

> We had such fun together. We laughed so much. Ann had a great sense of humor---she was a very funny woman.

Wayne Griffin passed away in 1981 and is buried near Ann, Nelson and Isabel Eddy in Hollywood Memorial Cemetery. When I visited with Elinor, she was serving as advisor for a series of CD recordings being made of her major works. In remembrance of the beautiful friendship they shared together, on the cover of Elinor's disc will be a replica of a watercolor painting by Millard Sheets which was given to the Griffins by Ann and Nelson Eddy. (Elinor Remick Warren passed away in June, 1991).

Sidney also remembers the house on Hudson. That's the house where Ann took a ride on one of his dogs. Although he didn't make the move with them, they always kept a room for him and he visited often. He laughs as he tells the story:

> I used to bring the dogs with me when I stopped over for a visit. One day when Mother opened the door, one of the dogs shot right between her legs, picked her up and carried her backwards the whole length of the house all the way to the living room where she was promptly dumped on the floor. Poor Mother, she was in shock and since she bruised easily, she was quite a sight for weeks to come. Needless to say---I left the dogs at home after that.

On April 27, 1950, Nelson and Ann journeyed to Philadelphia to accept an honorary degree of Doctor of Music from Temple University. Nelson laughingly joked that after receiving such a degree he may never be able to sing *Shortnin' Bread* again.

Finally, America began to relax. After many years of turmoil, a peaceful complacency settled over the country.

Life seemed to flow more easily and the gentle love ballads that filled the music stores during the early fifties seemed to match the mood. The bobbysoxers were getting a brief whiff of a new kind of rhythm as rock-n'roll began to grow stronger.

Nelson continued to be the greatest concert attraction that the nation has ever known. During interviews he would explain, "They don't like light opera anymore in Hollywood so here I am on the road." Louella Parsons continued her loyalty by stating, "Young people love Nelson Eddy. He always greets them in person and is ever available to answer their questions. He even helps the young people with their school work, although this is supposed to be a secret."

At the Academy Awards ceremony, Louis B. Mayer was honored for his distinguished service to the motion picture industry. But within months, Mayer was through at MGM. He was to be replaced by Dore Schary.

Chapter Twenty-One

As the war in Korea tapered off, the nation was lulled into an even deeper euphoria. No one wanted to be bothered by controversy. Our manners and style of dress began to project new images as a less decorous style of living altered our expectations. This new frivolity produced a decade of new fads such as hula hoops, Davy Crocket hats and telephone stuffing.

When Ann saw her first poodle-skirted teenager whirling a hula hoop about her hips, she was both infatuated and repelled. The transition from proper to profane left her totally perplexed. Refusing to relinquish the style and graciousness of her southern upbringing, she became known in later years as the last "Grand Dame" of Hollywood. Slacks were definitely out and white gloves remained the most important staple of her wardrobe. Ann was known to buy white gloves by the dozen and when they became smudged or torn she would gleefully toss them to "Chloe" the poodle. Sidney remembers Nelson exclaiming, "There goes another pair."

Television continued to edge its way into our homes where we gathered for laughter and respite from our troubles. While we stayed home, box offices across the country reeled from the shock of empty seats and unsold tickets. Theater agents were no longer able to guarantee performers a full house. The concerts, which had long been Nelson's main stay, simply dried up. Nelson tried to be philosophical. "Things have been over for me several times, but I just look for another open door. I've kind of hit a mid-life crisis." When Isabel asked him if he'd like to retire from show business, he emphatically told her, "Remove that word from your vocabulary".

Near the end of his final tour, he performed at the Alpine Village in Cleveland, Ohio. An electrical storm and power shortage caused all the lights to go out across town, but Nelson never missed a note. He calmly continued to perform with candles flickering from tables and no air conditioning. Although the room grew extremely hot and stuffy, the audience never moved. Throughout all his years of performing no one ever knew if he was sick or suffering. Nelson believed "the show must go on" and it usually did. When his beloved friend and teacher Edouard Lippe passed away, Nelson was deeply grieved. However, he continued his performance, dedicating the concert to his old friend.

The Lord's Prayer and *The Trumpet Shall Sound* from Handel's Messiah were frequent requests during his final concert tours, but the overflowing audiences were most thrilled with the encores from songs that he and Jeanette MacDonald had sung as "the team". Somehow, he felt there was a message in this for him.

In 1951, he recorded *With These Hands* with the popular Jo Stafford for Columbia Records. *Till We Meet Again* was on the flip side. "Jo's picking up some of my uptown trade and I'm picking up some of her jukebox trade, so we crooned together and decided to try a song," he explained. As it climbed to the top ten list, Nelson was as shocked as he was pleased.

But the most celebrated occasion was the long awaited arrival of their first grandchild. The birth of Victoria Alice was a joyous event and presented Nelson and Ann with a whole new flavor of life to savor.

Privately, he was still a very serious student of music. Sidney recalls that when he was home, Nelson sang a very boisterous "Boris Godunof" around the house. Instead of darkening with the years, his voice had actually lightened in texture, giving it a quality of freshness.

He also developed a love for popular music with its heavy orchestration and romantic tones. Nelson could relate to polished crooners like Eddie Fisher, Perry Como and Frank Sinatra. In fact when he appeared on the "Command Performance Show", he did an outstanding imitation of Frank Sinatra which brought down the house.

Privately his family and friends worried about his future. Where would he sing? What should he sing? But, to Nelson, continuing his career had other serious implications. As a husband and employer, he felt very strongly about his duty and responsibility for the welfare of others. It was imperative that he not let anyone down. Sidney remembers sitting at the dinner table one evening when Nelson told Ann, "I intend to keep you in the fashion I have kept you in from the day I married you and that's my decision." He also felt duty bound to provide for the well-being of his long time friend and accompanist as well as his personal staff. The decision to continue performing was a combination of practical need as well as creative desire.

When the news came from Rhode Island that Ginny had given birth to her first child, Wayne Linton Brown, it was a happy reprieve as the whole family joined in the celebration. But Ginny and Sidney clearly remember how Nelson suffered through this period of his life. He had only two choices open to him and he was frightened.

Audiences of the fifties wanted vitality and variety in a night club act. Could he give them that type of performance? And television was an uncharted territory with everyone clamoring to joint its ranks. But there was one thing that gave Nelson great pause; television made him nervous. Hadn't the critics reproached him for being stiff and wooden in his movies, and wouldn't the TV camera create the same image? In radio and movies, one could read a script, but television demanded the memorization of lines. Plus, the movie studios felt so threatened by television that they had begun to threaten anyone who went near the medium.

Nelson made his own feelings quite clear. "I'm fifty years old; who wants to see me jump around like a juvenile and make love to a pretty girl? Television is for younger people." Pushed by others, he talked at length to Milton Berle, Bob Hope and Jack Benny because they had successfully made the transition, but still, grave doubts remained. There was something that terrified him about the way television used people. He was afraid that if he washed up on television, he would be through with everything else. However, at the insistence of co-workers, he agreed to put his fears aside long enough to work with a producer on a half hour show for NBC called "Nelson Eddy's Backyard" which was to co-star Jan Clayton. Fate stepped in and the plans abruptly fell through, making the decision for him. He would appear as a guest on many television shows throughout the coming years, but his course would lead him into a far more risky venture---a nightclub act.

His friends found the whole idea unsettling, even distasteful. Could anyone who knew Nelson Eddy possibly imagine him singing Tin Pan Alley on the dance floor of a nightclub? Elinor Griffin remembers:

> Ann mentioned that Nelson was considering a nightclub act. I became really upset because I could not perceive him in that kind of arena. I remember telling Ann that it was such a shame to give up the concerts and I'll never forget her reply. She said, "It's the concerts that gave him up!"

Ask anyone who has worked the nightclub circuit and they will tell you that it is a very tricky, very risky business. You become extremely intimate with the audience and if you're bothered by the clatter of dishes or an occasional rowdy drunk, then it won't work. A nightclub act doesn't allow for a bad performance---everything counts. Most of Nelson's close associates thought he had undertaken an impossible task, that he'd never adjust. They desperately tried to talk him out of it. But the real Nelson Eddy, the witty and charming singer as he was known to family and friends, knew he could adjust. There was a lot of ham in Nelson. He liked to make people laugh and he loved to hear them applaud. He thought that the nightclub circuit would provide a lot of fun along with the intimacy he craved from an audience.

It was Ted who was the most rattled. "Aren't we crazy to try this? Making a jump from concert hall to nightclub stage might be suicide," he bemoaned. But Nelson held firm. Years of singing the concert circuit had given him the belief that he possessed an infallible instinct that leads the audience to become one with him. Granted, they were entering foreign territory, but Nelson was armed with class, charm and an unmatchable artistry.

Nelson knew himself well. Few singers had ever sung to such a heterogeneous audience and been so successful. His spontaneous temperament and fun had charmed thousands, and he sincerely believed that in the intimacy of a room filled with people, he became the best of what he was. Having finally made his decision, he bounced back to life with an abundance of energy. When Allen Young asked him to make a guest appearance on his television show a few weeks later, Nelson appeared amazingly relaxed and quickly put everyone at ease. He later noted that he even surprised himself. The show was so successful that he was asked to come back for the following segment. This was to be the start of many TV appearances over the years. As a guest, he enjoyed himself immensely, but he was never sorry for by-passing television for the nightclub circuit.

Chapter Twenty-Two

On January 21, 1953, a very nervous Nelson Eddy prepared to make his nightclub debut at Tops in San Diego, California. What transpired was an enhanced version of his performance twenty years ago when he was first "discovered". The ebullient Mr. Eddy was still in perfect harmony with his universe. "Variety" proceeded to take out a full page ad which headlined:

> EXPLOSIVE NEW ACT: Nelson Eddy, veteran of films, concerts and stage required less than one minute to put a jam-packed audience in his hip pocket in one of the most explosive openings in this cities nightery history. A simple unpremeditated gesture did the trick. Preceding his first show, Don Howard, KSDO's disc jockey at the night club, introduced Nelson Eddy and promptly started to leave the floor. Eddy strode on and pulled Howard back. Smiling broadly, he shook his hands and thanked him for the introduction. In this simple gesture of warmth, Eddy endeared the crowd before he had even started to sing. They liked him personally as a warm human being, something he had never seemed to be in his long career in other medias. The austerity had disappeared along with the stony faced singing mountie of the past. He was in truth a different Nelson Eddy. Nelson is a polished performer of surprising depth and feeling. Once more he sends us exactly what nightery freight payers want. In this case he gave sincerity, sentiment, showmanship and a sterling voice. He has them all. This can't miss.

To Nelson it was the same delivery he had given his audiences for thirty-five years. He did what he believed he was born to do---sing! It was a different stage, but the same enigmatic intertwining of voice and soul. Even Ted agreed the Tops debut was a grand affair.

As a professional showman, Nelson fine tuned his songs and comedy skits to play to the small supper clubs around the country. No one was more shocked than Nelson when he was called to perform for one month running at the Sahara Hotel, the largest show palace in Vegas---the big time! Never one to miss a challenge, he accepted with full knowledge that this was to be a "make it or break it" performance. He had precious little time to prepare. He knew the show needed work. It had to be bigger and better.

He needed more fluff, a "grabber". Ted was in no condition to be creative. His head was still spinning from the opening night at Tops and now he had to face the Sahara. The three of them were near desperation when Ann saved the day. She quietly suggested, "How about a female singer, a few duets?" The image immediately clicked in Nelson's mind. Memories of Jeanette and their shared duets came flowing back. He knew instinctively that it was the perfect way to bring familiarity to the audience.

He told Sidney, "I'm not looking for a partner; I just need someone who has a lovely voice and is very presentable to sing the duet in *Indian Love Call.* Nelson knew he had to move fast so he would have ample time to rehearse. On a wing and a prayer, he set up auditions telling himself all the while that it was no big deal. Just one song and that's that. He quickly made up his mind to offer the job to a young unknown. She accepted on the spot which left him little time to discuss the details with his lawyer so he decided to stop over and see if he needed legal papers. No sooner had he entered the lawyer's office than a call came for him. Someone had charged a large sum of money at a local department store. The store wanted to know if he would accept the charges. Nelson, perplexed, inquired as to who had made the charges only to discover it was his new singer. Without missing a beat, he refused the charges and revoked his offer. No one ever knew how serious his predicament was. He had rewritten the entire show and timed it perfectly for the new skits. Now he had no singer.

Gale Sherwood had just returned from a tour of "Desert Song". As a trained opera singer, she had been performing since childhood and was a seasoned professional in both film and stage acting. Her agent suggested she audition for Nelson as an interim until the next show started touring. It was the perfect filler.

The gods had blessed Gale with an over abundance of good looks, personality and talent. She was far older in maturity then her twenty-three years belied and was well-versed in the harsh realities of the entertainment world. Gale recalls her fateful meeting with Nelson.

> My mother was far more elated about it than I was. I walked into the audition with a very businesslike attitude and Nelson was utterly charming. He disarmed me by his gentle honesty. No wonder my mother was so excited, I thought to myself. Suddenly, I became very nervous. After all, this man was an artist of great magnitude. I relaxed a bit and sang a few songs. He graciously offered me the job. I was famished and went straight into the hotel restaurant and ordered a big plate of dollar size pancakes with butter. At a skinny 5'9", I could really put the food away. As I was leaving, Nelson caught up with me and suggested we discuss the show over breakfast. As luck would have it, we sat at the same table and the same waiter knowingly asked, "May I take your order Miss?" Relieved he hadn't given me away, I whispered, "Just

something light; raisin toast and tea, please." Nelson never knew.

Born in Hamilton, Ontario, Canada, Gale came to Hollywood as a young child in 1939 with her mother to study voice and dance. By the age of eleven, she was appearing in such movies as "They Shall Have Music" with Jasha Heifetz, "Let's Make Music" with Bob Crosby, and "Song of My Heart", the biography of Tchaikovsky.

> Meeting Nelson was proof to me that everything my mother had taught me still existed. Nelson invited my mother and me to dinner. Ann was wonderful. She never missed anyone's anticipation. The maid brought in finger bowls with petals of fresh roses floating in them. "Oh, Ann, isn't that lovely," I cried. "Well, what dear?" she asked. It was all so natural to her, she didn't think it was special. She was so terribly polished, so observant. We had such a beautiful evening. We prepared for the following week's show. Suddenly, everything was fait accompli!

During rehearsals, Gale saw an even more effervescent Eddy. Away from the lights he was a perfectly mannered, reserved gentleman, but on stage he had an aura that no amount of Hollywood coaching could improve upon. Gale added: "There was such character in his face, depth in his smile and a zing in his step."

When Gale mentioned his sex appeal, he looked totally perplexed. "What sex appeal, I don't know anything about it. Maybe you have it, you're pretty enough. But whatever it is, I don't think I have it."

With his energy and perseverance he overcame becoming a has-been. Neither Nelson nor Gale had ever performed in the nightclub environment before; both were apprehensive. Ted, on the other hand, was still frightened to death. Of all of them, Gale had the least to lose because she perceived the opportunity as a temporary job.

Chapter Twenty-Three

Opening night at the Sahara gave them all a case of frazzled nerves. The room was packed with a lively crowd as Nelson began to weave his lyrical spell. The audience never took their eyes off him. Even Ted was a big hit on solo piano. Then, as rehearsed, Gale poised herself on a rock upstage ready to give out with "You hoo hoo" to Nelson's "When I'm calling you". A very abbreviated Indian costume complimented her tall slender body. Nelson stood a few feet away from her with his arms outstretched, and as she started to move gracefully towards him off the rock, at that tender moment when they were both singing the duet, she suddenly lost her balance. She nearly toppled to the floor in the midst of a very high note. Instead of trying to carry it off legitimately, she clowned and came on stage with a Groucho Marx walk. The audience loved it! They roared with laughter as the Indian Maiden quickly recovered and waddled over to her waiting "lover". It didn't take Nelson long to realize that Gale Sherwood was not just a show girl who could sing, but a very talented singer who could play musical comedy as well. She could dance, sing and handle lines. By the time they reached the Copacabana in New York, Nelson had already made his decision. He asked her to stay with him and she delightedly accepted.

Once their relationship passed the beginning stages, no contracts were signed. Through all their 39 years of working together, Nelson and Ted had only a verbal agreement between them and now Gale was accepted into the family the same way. It was purely a matter of stay-if-you-want or go-if-you-want. Money was treated with the same casual trust. Whatever they needed, he was willing to give.

> I will never forget how he and Ann lent me the money to buy a new car. It was a black mustang. And as a gift, Ann had a beautiful leopard throw rug and pillow made for the car. Once a month, I paid Nelson money towards the car and he didn't like it. He would say, "I know what you make. I pay you, remember? You've got to support your mother, so you can't possibly afford to give me this car payment." When I paid off the debt, he was truly impressed.

Transition from concert star to nightclub entertainer wasn't easy. Nelson retained The Music Corporation of America as his agents. One of the key elements of the new act was that it was in no way to be reminiscent of his concerts.

Ann played a big part in the choice of costumes and makeup. She and Gale would try out all kinds of new ideas on Nelson and he in turn would try his skits out on them. Gale remembers Ann telling Nelson, "It won't fly, dear," and he'd immediately change the script.

Both Nelson and Gale lived by the morals and manners of their strict upbringing. They were both very gracious people. Gale believes that's why they understood each other so well. "We were fish out of water then and would appear to be even more so if he were here today."

When they appeared at the Copacabana in New York, Nelson caught a terrible cold. The doctor felt that were he to sing all the songs, he might damage his vocal cords; so Gale sang the solos and Nelson sang very lightly in their duets. The sketches were so funny that the audience never knew he was sick. Even with all the problems, their appearance at the Copa drew rave reviews, and it was then that Ted realized that the nightclub act was really going to work. Gale loved Ted's quiet confirmation of their success; "We're really good," he beamed.

Gale reflected on their time together:

> I learned so much from Nelson. He was so dependable, so responsible, so true to his word. If he said it was---then it was. We respected each other. I remember in the beginning of our act together, he wouldn't let me wear a form-fitting dress. He preferred antebellum dresses. I'd say in a mischievous way, "You let me show my legs at the end of the show. Besides, I can't see the mike chord under my hoops and smaller dresses are easier to pack." "But they're more expensive to buy," he laughed. I got to wear the form fitting dresses and Nelson loved them. That's how we usually solved our problems.

Elinor Griffin recalls that Gale was very charming to her and to all of Nelson's friends. She remembers what a very big part of both Ann's and Nelson's lives Gale became. Ann always referred to Gale as "our Gale".

Nelson, Ted and Gale continued to fly high. Their success was celebrated over and over again at each performance. Gale could not imagine how anything could mar the perfect harmony of their happiness. She'd never experienced Nelson's past fame and even though she understood the magnitude of his stardom, she was unprepared for the extreme loyalty of his fans.

Gale remembers that on her third nightclub appearance with Nelson, a reporter asked what it was like to be in Jeanette MacDonald's shoes. Gale tried to answer with a little humor "I wear a nine and she only wears a five."

Nelson and Ann were well aware of the comparisons being made and continued to give her encouragement and support. In the beginning, Gale remained somewhat aloof from the public allowing Nelson to speak for both of them. She respected and trusted him implicitly.

> He was always a gentlemen, honest and concerned for my welfare. In one instance, there was a quip in "Variety" about my drinking which wasn't true. Nelson could see how upset I was. He didn't drink either; one martini with a skewer of olives was his usual limit, but he realized far more than I just what we were up against.
>
> I had no hold on the public's memory. I had no idea just how brutal and unrelenting the fans could be. In the beginning I was either compared to Jeanette and left wanting or totally ignored by Nelson's legion of fans.

Nelson disliked the way the interviewers treated Gale, but their act was new and he felt that in time things would improve.

> I remember Nelson and Ann telling me, "The press has to be the press." But it was terribly disheartening. The attitude about publicity during our show business days was---hope they spell the name right. We were all very cognizant that we could not control what the reporters or the fans would say about us, and we tried to overcome the rumors by being rather cavalier.

Nelson wrote every script for every performance with suggestions here or there from Ted, Ann or Gale. Gale describes the tremendous pressures and problems of the nightclub circuit in those days:

> It was especially hard to do a nightclub act, because you were so very close to the audience. They see you and you see them and they watch every move you make. You never know who's going to be in the audience, or what kind of audience you must perform to. There were so many other problems to contend with, we felt that our efforts to put the act on night after night were monumental.
>
> Today entertainers have people who set up the clubs for them, handle hated travel arrangements, and even test their equipment. Even a star's meals are specially prepared. We had all the ticketing to do, the reservations, preparing the room, finding appropriate food, and still we had the energy to do the show. Never mind the mikes that were broken, the bands which couldn't play our music and the hundreds of meals left uneaten.

Jeanette and Gene Raymond often came to see Nelson's act. Even though they had taken different paths, Jeanette and Nelson remained friends throughout the years. Whenever Nelson played Los Angeles or New York City, if Jeanette was in town at the time, she always made it a point to be in front on Nelson's opening night. Nelson, in turn, would always send a warm congratulatory note to Jeanette for her performances.

It was obvious by the continuous number of sold out audiences and rave reviews that Nelson had made the transition into the post-war generation. At a time in his life when most men would have been content to retire, Nelson was going full blast. Midway in his third career, he had solidly established himself as a nightclub entertainer. He estimated that he had sung *Rose Marie* between 6,000 and 7,000 times.

"Success extolled a high price from us," Gale recalls.

In order to survive the pressure, each of us had a job. I signed us into the hotels and made sure that the rooms were ready. I always ordered fruit for me and the Saturday Review for Nelson. Ted was in charge of the music. Nelson handled all of the bookings, schedules and scripts. It took a lot to get Nelson mad, but when his room wasn't prepared properly, that would do it. The biggest problem was finding a restaurant open after our last show at 3:00 A.M.

Very slowly and ever so surely, we began to settle into a routine. We were a team. Most important to me was that the fans accepted me.

Chapter Twenty-Four

Sidney was having his own problems working for MGM back in Hollywood.

> I was producing films and feeling quite proud of myself, but I could see the beating that the studios were taking because of television and I thought there must be alternatives. During a seminar taught by Mr. Moskovitz, the Vice President of CBS, he talked at length about the possibility of using television to sell film and I thought this was a brilliant idea. It was an incredible marketing tool because television was now reaching the adult buying head. I was so sure of the success of this idea that, after the seminar, I wrote to Nickolas Schenk, the Chairman of MGM, and told him that I had an idea which would revolutionize Hollywood. He agreed to meet with me.
>
> You see, the studios refused to believe that television was as strong as it was. They blamed their declining profits on the new recreational pursuits ushered in by the fifties such as bowling alleys and golfing ranges. They refused to recognize television as a friend. The attitude around the studio lot was "we'll destroy television". So when I entered Mr. Schenk's office for our meeting, I said, "You may fire me for this idea," and he answered, "I might!"
>
> "We should be using television to market our films," I explained. I went on to present all the data Mr. Moskovitz had given me and it was pretty heavy stuff...success ratios and all the marketing facts. Three days later I was fired.
>
> My dad had warned me not to get involved but Nelson disagreed. Nelson had refused to be beaten

> down by Hollywood and felt I should speak my peace. We had all seen so many people whipped by the system, I chose to speak my feelings.
>
> In retrospect, I am proud of standing up. I have never regretted my decision, but it was a long time before I ever worked in Hollywood again. The studios were down the tubes and I knew it was time to move on too. My friend and agent, Al Manuel was doing well in building construction, so I went back to engineering and formed a partnership with two other builders. We found success by specializing in the construction of modern homes. I've been at it now for thirty years.

By the end of 1954 life had a new flow. Ann's happiness was directly connected to Nelson's; therefore, she relished his new found career. She would silence anyone who dared to question Nelson's choices by stating firmly, "He's so happy."

But the joy was all too brief, because the public was restless. A new nightclub act and a beautiful new singing partner; surely there must be more to this than meets the eye. Nelson held firm to his old beliefs and continued in his refusal to give the public any information about his private life. Left to fill in the silences with conjectures and innuendos of their own making---the fans wrote the script.

Gale remembers the rumors as though they happened yesterday:

> We were amazed by some of the rumors about us. Anyone who knew Ann Eddy was aware she was not only a strong woman but an involved wife and was the world to Nelson. Indeed! They were the team!
>
> Had there been anything amiss, I would not have lasted. Nelson would never have allowed his years of dedicated work and spotless reputation to have been

> destroyed. Bad publicity was the last thing we needed or deserved.
>
> Of course, we kissed every night on the stage---it was part of the show. The much publicized "Belly-button" controversy came about due to my appearance in a revealing harem costume, while singing songs from "Desert Song". The comedy skit called for a jewel to be glued in a strategic spot...the belly-button, which was rather bold in the fifties and frankly, it hurt! During the kiss at the end of the song, Nelson would remove the jewel, and while bowing he would show it to the audience. It was quite a surprise and a great finale. Today it would be considered far from risque.

The nightclub act continued to play the best clubs across the country. But, while Nelson and Gale performed to their generation, a whole new sound was being introduced on radio. The music was characterized by amplified instruments with a heavy beat and the words were sung by untrained voices. When Elvis Presley captured the younger generation with his wild mix of country rhythm and blues, the record industry realized things would never quite be the same.

The first time Nelson saw Elvis wiggle and grunt, he knew he would never be the same. Gale recalls that she and Ann watched as Nelson sat entranced by Elvis. His only words were "Oh God"!

The audiences which flocked to Nelson's show found rock and roll music to be obscene and insulting. They had no understanding of the beat which would rock the nation. Gale believes that Nelson gave his audiences the dignity and graciousness they needed in a world which was drastically changing.

> He was much more a beautifully handsome man in person---he had the carriage and deportment of a god. He was perfectly built and his suits were tailored within an inch of his body. He had beautiful thick wavy hair and blue eyes as big as saucers. His eyes were dark sapphire blue, and he had perfect pitch. What more can you ask? We used to tease him all the time by cooing, "and he sings too."
>
> He was fastidious to a fault. We were always properly attired. While the younger generation adopted shorts, I wore hats and gloves, and never slacks.

Nelson and Gale became one of the most popular acts ever to play the nightclub circuit. He designed the show to be versatile. He mixed the nostalgia with the modern, calling his he-man songs, "muscle songs". *Tramp, Tramp, Tramp, Song of the Mounties, The Vagabond Song* and *Stout-hearted Men* were the lusty songs by which he had long been identified.

Gale laughingly recalls:

> The theme of our interviews were always the same. We were the most boring people in show business. We never missed a plane, a train, a boat, or a bus.
>
> Nelson was a worrier and a true perfectionist. In fourteen years, the only time we missed a show was when Nelson was hospitalized with pneumonia. Jack Jones filled in for us.

Even though the act was a great success, nothing could change the minds of Nelson's oldest and dearest friends. In truth, they never accepted the night club act as a part of his stellar career.

When Elinor, a famous composer herself, heard Nelson sing the popular songs so prevalent in his nightclub act, it would cause her great discomfort. Ann would often invite Elinor and Wayne to the clubs in California, but they found it difficult to share in Nelson's new found love. They wanted to hear him sing the Brahms and Wagner he loved so much. In their minds, Nelson was so much better than that. He was an opera singer and hearing him sing *Love and Marriage* just didn't seem right. They preferred to visit Nelson and Ann in the privacy of their home away from the public eye where Nelson would once again sing his beloved opera.

Bobby Armbruster had a long talk with Nelson about the new act and is convinced to this day that Nelson loved it.

> I never could feel comfortable hearing Nelson sing the tin pan alley pattern, but I knew he truly loved the freedom and the fun he was having. He finally had the freedom to do what he wanted. He had put away "the serious musician". No matter what he chose to do, he did it with the same gusto and determination that had taken him successfully through his career. Still, it was most definitely hard for me to forget his concert style and image.

The big white Monterey home was becoming too much for Nelson and Ann, but they remained because of the Griffins. When he was home between tours, the Griffin children were always around to play with "Uncle Nelson".

Elinor recalls a typical Nelson story with deep affection.

> One of our boys had left his bicycle on the front lawn once too often and Wayne decided to hide the bike in the Eddy garage to teach him a lesson. Our son was terribly distraught over the "theft" of his prized possession. After only two days, Nelson couldn't bear

it any longer. Muttering that "things had gone too far, and after all a boy should have his bicycle," he wheeled it out of the garage and into our son's gleeful hands.

Chapter Twenty-Five

Life was indeed an ever changing process. The once handsome golden boy now stood stately and debonair, and as the nightclub act continued to prove successful, family and friends adjusted to Nelson's newest image. Nothing had really changed. He was still the ever-striving perfectionist, quick to demand the best of himself.

Nelson's new success brought back all the demands of his early popularity, and his personal staff grew with the demands. There were multitudes of scripts to type and the ever growing correspondence to answer. He searched for a personal secretary whom he could trust and feel comfortable with and found her in Mildred Hudson. She too would remain by his side until his death.

Mildred was a wonderful earthy soul full of life, and Nelson loved her. He would try out a script on her and if she let out a good belly laugh, he knew he had it. Mildred wrote about Nelson, "He was a man you could be quiet with---not bored---just quiet. He would set out to disarm anyone who was infatuated with him. He only wanted the happy comfortable feeling of friendship."

Whenever he could, Nelson escaped into his paintings. His style became very whimsical and free after he started the nightclub act. Mildred always said, "Nelson's personality became alive in his art work."

One of Nelson's "Ha Ha" paintings which he did during the early fifties hangs on the wall of Sidney's and Janine's home today. It's a bird's eye view of his studio half way down the hill. Nelson drew it as a little fat laughing two-story bungalow with a jagged picture window for a gaping mouth and the sides bulging with laughter. The trees around the house have lolly-pop heads.

One day Gale walked in while Nelson was working on a light-hearted sculpture. His art work always depicted such warmth and humor about people and life in general that Gale commented on its message. "This is just how I feel", he smiled. "I've enjoyed my life and I've really enjoyed these last few years of my life".

As Nelson's travel schedule grew even more complex and Ann's arthritis continued to trouble her, the Eddy's knew it was time to move. The house was simply too big for them. They found the perfect house in West Bel Aire. Elinor and Wayne had dinner at the Eddys' new home at 166 Ashdale Place three days after they moved in. Nelson loved his new home because it had several acres of brush and trees. "I got a couple of acres with a lot of brush, bush and miserable terrain. Little by little, I work on it and build retaining walls and rocks and put in new hedges and plant new trees. I think it will go on forever, because I can't imagine it every being finished." As the nightclub act took them further across the country, gardening became one of his only escapes.

As the years continued, Nelson, Gale, and Ted worked the supper clubs, hotels, conventions and theater-in-the-round. They loved the versatility, and above all, they loved the closeness of an audience. Nelson liked to set Gale up for his one liners which were always crowd pleasers.

Gale remembers:

> Life became very routine for us. The hero worship and franticness that Nelson had experienced earlier in his career were now only memories. He could walk down the street without being mobbed. Nelson and Ted were great walkers, but they would go in different directions. Nelson enjoyed visiting museums and art

> galleries. Ted liked seeing the city and its people. I didn't exercise as I danced every night and preferred to stay in my hotel room and write letters, read or see to my hair and nails. For the most part, we led very separate lives. We never lived in each other's pockets. But at 4:45 every afternoon we met faithfully for rehearsals and dinner. When it came to the performance, we were all perfectionists.

When Nelson was home and could relax, he and Ann entertained. He loved intimate parties with small groups of friends like the Griffins, Doris Kenyon, the Meredith Willsons, the Dennis O'Keefes and the Lloyd Nolans. Lloyd characterized Nelson as, "a brilliant conversationalist, generous, witty and warm. At those small get togethers, Nelson would oblige us with song after song."

Many of Nelson's old movie star friends came to see his performance. Kathryn Grayson was amazed that as he grew older Nelson remained such a perfectionist. Many of the older performers became sloppy with age, but not Nelson.

He didn't always sing the nightclub patter either. Once in awhile, he would break rank and sing a song more reminiscent of days gone by, his baritone as strong and distinctive as ever. At Suttmillers in Dayton, Ohio, Nelson and Gale drew capacity crowds even during their mid-week performances. On one occasion, Nelson left the mike and began to walk around the room with his hands in his pockets. All of a sudden, he began singing *Shenandoah* with such terrific impact it was as though he was still at the microphone. The audience was spellbound. From that point on, he often included *Shenandoah* in the act.

He continued to make guest appearances on television throughout the next ten years. He appeared on shows such as "The Colgate Comedy Hour", "The Bob Hope Show",

"The MGM Parade", "The Edgar Bergen Show", and "What's My Line". He loved to ad lib and act out character skits. His favorite guest appearance was with Bob Hope. Bob and Nelson were quite a pair; they got along famously. Bob described Nelson as "one of the most delightful men in show business". Nelson received critical acclaim for his portrayal of a "Zoot Suited Be-Bopster" on Bob's show. Nelson also appeared on the "Spike Jones Show", "Jukebox Jury", "The Big Record" with Patti Page, "Tennessee Ernie Ford Show", "Rosemary Clooney Show", "Jack Parr Show", "Ed Sullivan Show", "Dinah Shore Show", "The Today Show", and "Hollywood Palace".

He appeared on "This is Your Life" when Jeanette MacDonald was the guest of honor. He almost gave away the whole surprise for Jeanette when she recognized his car in the studio parking lot. He and Jeanette did the "The Big Parade Show" and "The Big Record Show". He made other guest appearances on "The Merv Griffin Show", "Make Room For Daddy", "Rusty Draper", "The USO Christmas Show" and "Mike Douglas".

Nelson gave in to television only once. He played the lead in Max Liebman's production of "Desert Song" in 1955. It co-starred Gale Sherwood with Otto Kruger, John Conte, Salvatore Baccalone, Viola Essen, Bambi Lynn and Rod Alexander. He had never done a major show on stage or television before and the techniques were all new to him. He was pained by the reviews and disappointed in his own image. He felt he had tried too hard and had failed in his efforts to capture the essence of the dashing dare-devil lover he portrayed. Gale had come across beautifully, but it proved to him that unless he was free to be himself---he set a dismal example of contrived acting.

He and Gale returned to the success of the nightclub circuit. But the pace became even more demanding and his temper was quick to flare. Slowly, sacrifices had to be made. Sidney recalls, "When Nelson gave up the horses of which he was so fond, he was depressed for weeks." His painting and sculpture were also neglected as his time became filled with the never ending script writing and rehearsals. Although Nelson seldom complained, there was a noticeable sadness about him whenever he couldn't find time to paint or sculpt.

He cherished his family. Because he was on the road so much, he was especially touched by all the special occasions families celebrate. When Sidney and Mary Alice presented the Eddy's with their second granddaughter, Roxanne Louise, Nelson and Ann came with their arms loaded with bountiful gifts. Sidney recalls, "He never took anything for granted---he appreciated every moment."

Bill Eddy wrote to Isabel in 1955, "I spent quite a long time with Nelson on this last visit. He has everything to be on top of the world about, but he seemed so withdrawn and depressed. What's wrong with our boy?"

Chapter Twenty-Six

Nelson continued the grind of a two-show a day nightclub act and rave reviews continued to follow him. On October 21, 1956, the Kansas City Star wrote: "Nelson Eddy, widely known singing star and his attractive singing partner have one of the best acts in the business. Everything they do is right. Audiences can't get enough of them. We can describe Nelson as zingy." And as Gale attested, "Nelson played the easy-going pro on stage, but off stage he was the ultimate organizer. He always carried a complete travel schedule for the next several months which included flight numbers and departure times, everything was written down and scheduled appropriately, every bill was recorded and paid on time."

Tom Cooper, a popular night club entertainer during the fifties remembers appearing at the same club with Nelson and Gale.

> There were 800 people packed into the Colonial Inn at St. Petersburg, Florida, to see their act. It was exhilarating and the audience loved them. After the show we spent a few hours talking together. I remember how extremely modest Nelson was about his talent. He often deferred to Gale's youth and talent being the reason people came to see them. He was upset that evening because the Lake Club in Springfield, Illinois had never paid him for their performance. It really bothered him that people were so unethical. To my recollection, their show was the best nightclub act in the midwest during the fifties.

Bill used to visit Nelson and Gale whenever he could. Sometimes Marguerite came, but usually he would just show up unannounced. Gale recalls:

> We always nicknamed him Colonel Eddy. He was a great character and Nelson was the spitting image of his father. One day when we arrived for rehearsal at the Waldorf Astoria, who should also arrive but Colonel Eddy. He came in dragging a sack of dirty quahogs with sea water dripping from them. Nelson took one look and exclaimed, "Oh my God", and walked over to the other side of the stage smothering his laughter. I jumped off the stage and gently steered Dad Eddy through the check out area and downstairs into the kitchen. The chef took one look at the dripping sack, peeked inside and announced, "These will make great chowder!" Dad Eddy replied with his New England accent, "Yup, but I'm doin' the cookin'". And sure enough he and the chef made an absolutely delicious soup. He was a most adorable and charming man with a great sense of humor. When Dad Eddy came to visit he would walk in and say, "Well son, where's my Old Grandads?" This was a long standing tradition.
>
> I knew that Dad Eddy and Isabel kept in touch all through the years. There was genuine concern between them for each other's welfare and Nelson was happy about that.
>
> There are so many memories. Nelson's family were all so wonderful, especially Ann. I learned the art of gift giving from that marvelous lady; she was immensely generous. It was not unusual for me to receive thirty gifts for Christmas. Plus, Ann and Nelson showered presents on my mother and sister.
>
> Isabel and I were very good friends. She regularly invited me to tea and was always interested in our act. I would bring along my new gowns to show her, and

Gale Sherwood

The Nightclub Act
Nelson and Gale

Ted, Gale and Nelson
Vancouver, B.C., Canada

Nelson and Gale - charity ballgame, Reno, Nevada

"The Final Finale ended with 'The Kiss'. We once figured that in 15 years we kissed 5000 times....but we never got it right!" -Gale Sherwood

Bell Telephone Hour, 1952 - Thelma Cohen, next to Nelson, and fan club members

On tour

Toledo, Ohio, 1958 - Gale and Nelson, Ted at piano

"The Ed Sullivan Show"

Nelson's and Ann's home in L.A. across from the Griffins

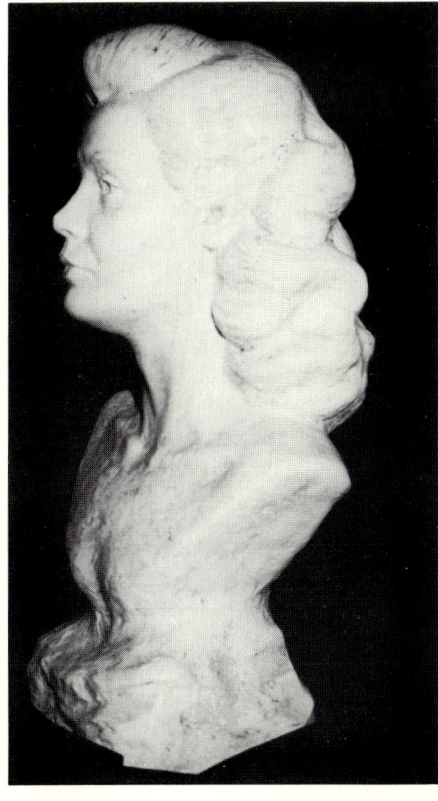

Busts of Gale by Nelson

Honolulu cruise

Gale, Nelson, Ann, Ted, Helen

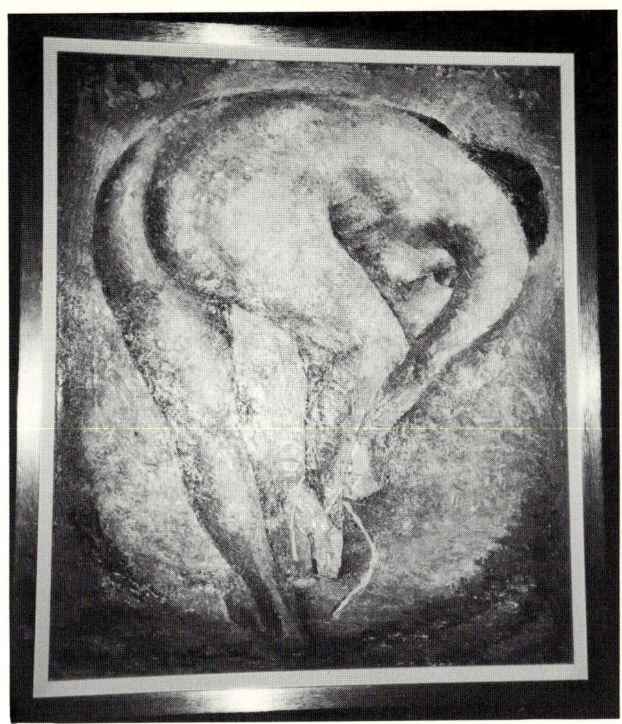

Oil by Nelson of nude

Oil by Nelson of Gale

Bronze sculpture by Nelson

Nelson and Bill with Elliott (4 1/2) and Wayne (11), January 1964

Lloyd, Bill, Marguerite, a friend, Ginny, Nelson, Elliott, Wayne
Ted took the picture in January, 1964

CONSOLATION—Ann Denitz Eddy, widow of Nelson Eddy, is comforted by Gene Raymond after service.
Times photo by John Malmin

Gene Raymond, Sidney and Ann

Dr. Swan, Ann Eddy, Dr. Gross
Donation of Nelson's music to Occidental College

Nelson Eddy Room, Occidental College

> we would talk about the next engagement. Best of all, she liked me to give her a manicure. She was a proud and beautiful lady. I enjoyed making her happy. After Isabel passed away, Nelson gave me her elegant gold bracelet and matching ring with pearls. She had wanted me to have them, and I wear them often today.
>
> On Tuesdays, we rehearsed at Nelson's home. Ann knew how much I liked dungeness crab, so after rehearsal, we'd have a feast! Helen, Ted, Nelson, Ann and I went to the study, and there, surrounded by San Francisco sourdough bread would be crab galore with herbed mayonnaise for dipping. Nelson mixed a perfect pitcher of martinis and it was all served on the Chinese porcelain dishes they liked so much. Suffice to say, I loved rehearsals!
>
> We had some wonderful trips together. Helen and Ann would join us in the big cities like New Orleans or Atlanta where Ann had family. Then we'd take time to shop and visit together. In the later years it became too difficult for Ann to travel. She had Isabel and her parents to care for.

Jeanette also enjoyed success on the nightclub circuit. She and Gene made several television shows together and, whenever she could, she performed in summer stock. Her hectic schedule continued until a slight heart condition began to worsen. When Nelson and Gale opened at the Los Angeles Statler, in the summer of 1957, Jeanette was at ringside and later visited back stage. It was then that she and Nelson agreed to record a nostalgic revival of the music most closely associated with their names for RCA Victor Records.

Isabel had suffered from heart problems in the past few years as well. Nelson refused to consider her condition as serious. He believed his mother would always be there for him. He commented to his friends, "No matter how old you are, a mother is a unique person, and the older you are, the more you appreciate her." When Isabel died at 5:30 AM on December 19, 1957, of cardiovascular disease at St. John's hospital in San Monica, California, Nelson grieved terribly. At times he was unable to control his sorrow. "It was a difficult time," Gale remembers. "They had meant so much to one another. To the public he appeared very strong and stoic, but in private he was terribly distraught. He knew that the show must go on, and in truth, the performances helped him to get through her death."

Ann remained in California and waited for Nelson to help her in closing Isabel's house. They spent several days going through boxes of mementos that they had stored at Isabel's years ago. In one box Nelson came across a birthday card from his mother which she had sent him years earlier. He always cherished it. Today it lies in a locked suitcase with many of Nelson and Ann's beloved memories. Sidney and Janine often spend time going through these mementos together.

The following year, on March 10, 1958, Ann's mother passed away. She had been living in a sanitarium in Garden Grove, California. The loss was painful and again, they grieved together.

Jeanette and Nelson's album "Jeanette MacDonald and Nelson Eddy Favorites in HiFi" was released in 1959. As the album moved up to Gold Record status, Jeanette's health began to seriously deteriorate. In August she entered Georgetown Hospital for treatment.

In the midst of so much sorrow surrounding the family, an occasion for joy was enthusiastically embraced as Nelson became an uncle again. Ginny called very early on the morning of September 6th to announce the birth of Elliott Eddy Brown. Nelson told his father and Marguerite, "Ginny has accomplished something that I never did; she had children."

Nelson's nephews adored him. When Wayne Brown was about five years old, Ginny and Lloyd remember Wayne's delight upon seeing Nelson come through the door. "Hi, Uncle Nelson," he screamed as he ran up to him and threw his arms around him. And for Nelson the feelings were mutual. Ginny recalls, "He played with the boys whenever we were together. I remember how concerned he was for our welfare. He was always getting crank phone calls and so he seldom mentioned us publicly for fear something would happen to the boys. It was during this time that Nelson and I became much closer."

While home for a brief rest, Nelson decided to try his hand at song writing. The result was *Its Love, Love, Love,* released by Everest Records in 1960. It did quite well on the charts, but few people knew it was Nelson Eddy's music and lyrics. Sidney quipped, "Nelson thought it was the perfect song for that nice clean cut Pat Boone."

Nelson loved the way Vaughn Monroe sang. He couldn't get over the fact that Vaughn could make a legato line so naturally. Another favorite was Bob Newhart. Gale recalled that Nelson came to rehearsal one day talking about him. "Bob Newhart is one of the nicest people I have met in a long, long time. I wish I could know him better."

During the years of the night club act, Nelson's fan club remained close to him. They stayed with him for over twenty years and he felt they were the most wonderful and loyal people in the world.

Sidney and Ginny agree that the nightclub act gave Nelson the freedom he so desperately desired. On stage he was full of fun, wit, charm and naturalness and he continued to steal his audiences's hearts away. As the years passed, the fans learned to appreciate Gale and love her for the talented, animated entertainer she was. Above all, those closest to Nelson are ever grateful to her for her friendship and loyalty.

Chapter Twenty-Seven

The sixties wrought such terrible turbulence upon the country. It became a time of civil chaos, political assassinations, and defiance and hostility over the Vietnam War. Our mediocrity was suddenly shaken as anti-establishment sentiments crept into our settled lives. Through it all, Nelson and Ann remained loyal and duty bound to each other.

Gale remembers their love affair with tenderness.

> Ann was the perfect wife for Nelson. He'd call up and say, "Dear, I'm bringing home thirty people for dinner" and she'd calmly reply, "Fine darling, I'll be ready." Of course they had help, but she prepared most of it and would oversee each detail. During our tours, they talked every night on the phone and the letters flew back and forth. She'd cut out articles and I'd always see them laid out on Nelson's desk next to his scripts. They loved each other very much. They had special little sayings and meanings between them. She had health problems, but she seldom complained. She was always supportive of Nelson and almost always did what he wanted. She'd start laughing and say "You can't do that; you can't warm over a souffle". If something wasn't proper or appropriate she would take my arm and say, "But Gale, it doesn't go in the salad".

After touring in the United States and Mexico successfully for nine years, Nelson's agents scheduled a tour to Australia. He and Gale were excited by the new challenge and hoped to gain many new fans. But his agents warned that the audiences "down under" were not demonstrative by nature. Gale recalls their first visit as a "delightful surprise".

Nelson was sixty-one and Gale thirty-four when they made their debut in Sydney, Australia in 1962. The tour also included appearances in Brisbane and Adelaide. Instead of reserved, the audiences were warm and enthusiastic! By the time the newspapers and radio stations interviewed them---a love affair had been born. The fans were wonderful to Nelson and Gale. It was a case of mutual admiration for all concerned. Nelson, ever the self-analyst, viewed his reception with no pretensions. "I just want to please. I love working to people and their acceptance is our reward." The "rewards" continued as Nelson and Gale traveled across the country.

Ann found more time on her hands than she preferred. Always active in social and charitable activities, her arthritis began to hamper her involvement. She found it quite maddening that she couldn't move as quickly as she used to. She often felt at odds with the world and its ever changing pace. Part of her missed the excitement of modern times, yet she continued to hold on to the comfortable familiarity of old friends and treasured memories.

Short trips and shopping sprees with her beloved grandchildren, Victoria and Roxanne, helped to fill the void along with frequent visits with her sister Irene. She and Doris Kenyon often met for long leisurely lunches which stretched into the late afternoon. Elinor and Ann talked at least once a day and also visited often.

Nelson always included Ann in their plans for the Australia tours, but at the last minute, something would prevent her from going. It became a family joke, but when their plans were interrupted again, Nelson was visibly upset. He wanted Ann to experience Australia exactly as he had.

He knew she might not be able to make the trip if her health worsened and this deeply distressed him.

The Australian fans were so excited to see Nelson and Gale on their third visit, they threw orchids at their feet. The "Melody Express" toured for three weeks. Nelson and Gale often entertained the touring company at restaurants after the show. Carl Shafto who played lead trumpet on the 1964 tour remembers "Nelson has such consideration for his fellow workers and a complete devotion to his work." Before Nelson and Gale left Australia, a fourth visit was already in the plans and his depressed state of mind had been buoyed by their reception.

To all who knew him, Nelson was happy---he had reached an age of contentment, but he just couldn't stop working. During one interview, Nelson was asked "When are you going to retire?" He replied, "I can't even begin to think retirement. I don't think I'll ever retire. After all, I have three families to think about". Sidney believes, "Nelson felt too much responsibility. Even if he would have wanted to quit, he never could have."

As Nelson and Gale crossed the country, they made many new friends. The talk show hosts of late night radio loved to have them come over after their own show was finished. Gale remembers, "We would hop in a taxi and do a late show all over again."

"We had wonderful song fests," Gale recalls. "Nelson would spend the whole evening in song with friends like Lawrence Melchior, Robert Merrill or Helen Traubel. He never tired of singing."

Moxie Whitney was the orchestra conductor at the Royal York Hotel in Toronto, Ontario, Canada where Nelson and Gale made six appearances. He wrote in "The Shooting Star":

> During their second appearance, Nelson asked to conduct for a while. He went on stage and led the orchestra for three or four numbers, grinning at the audience the whole time.
>
> One of the things that impressed people at the Royal York was the way Nelson did his sitting-up exercises, knee bends, etc. during rehearsal. He was a very active man, and looking after his health was very important to him. Before the show he chewed gum to relieve the tension, since he no longer smoked. He was always very nervous before opening night and did not like to talk to anyone before he went on stage. It was always his desire to give the best performance that he could, and he dedicated himself to that purpose.

The nightclub act continued to draw record breaking audiences. Nelson's favorite line on stage became, "A woman walked up to me on the street and said, I know you. Weren't you Nelson Eddy?" In one of his interviews Nelson said, "I think I'm a bit mellower. I can't think of anything in my career I regret, but I remember the hysteria I used to attract. I use to get mad because I was so frightened by it and I didn't like it. But now I feel I am having fun. It's like the dessert after a good meal."

Ginny believes that these last few years were definitely Nelson's best. She vividly remembers the last time that all the Eddy's were together.

> It was a cool and wintery January day in 1964 while Nelson was appearing in Boston. Usually Nelson said his goodbyes at the elevator door of his hotel rather than coming downstairs to the lobby. However, during this particular visit, he not only came down to the lobby, but he walked out to the car with us. As we drove away, I looked back and he was still standing there watching us go. It made me stop and think. I

> had a compulsion to have Lloyd stop the car. I wanted to run back and tell him, "Take care of yourself---you're the only brother I've got," but the traffic was so heavy, we had to drive on.

Sidney had his own problems to work out. He and Mary Alice decided to divorce in 1962. The family was well aware of their many problems, and a form of relief set in when the decision to separate became final. It was only a short time before Sidney was introduced to Janine Briet and they quickly became friends. Nelson was very fond of Janine. She had been a singer in Paris, France. The first time she met Nelson she sang *Rose Marie* in French and won his heart forever.

Janine fondly recalls Nelson's generosity.

> Nelson called and asked me if I would help him pick out a strand of pearls for Ann's birthday. After much deliberation, we settled on two styles. One was a beautiful long strand and the other necklace was a shorter version of creamy cultured pearls. I explained to Nelson that the shorter style would be the most becoming on Ann and he agreed. However, he kept asking me if I really liked the other necklace as well. After we purchased the pearls for Ann, we stood outside the jewelry store admiring them. He then reached into his pocket, grinning broadly, as he handed me the other strand of pearls.

At sixty-four, the travel, rehearsals and constant performances began to take their toll on Nelson's health and mental energy. He desperately needed to rest, but the time between tours never seemed long enough.

"I particularly remember Jeanette's death," Sidney recalls, "because Nelson had just returned from a bone-tiring three weeks. He was working in the music room when the call came about Jeanette's death."

Jeanette had flown to Houston in preparation for open-heart surgery, but her condition deteriorated quickly. She passed away on January 14, 1965. Nelson was an honorary pall bearer along with former Presidents Eisenhower and Truman, Ronald Reagan, Spencer Tracy, Tom Clark, Earl Warren and Alfred Hitchcock. Gale and Ann went to the funeral together where they met the Griffins and Bobby Armbruster. Nelson's dear friend, Lloyd Nolan delivered the eulogy.

Nelson was sickened by the circus atmosphere surrounding Jeanette's funeral. The publicists had set up huge loudspeakers which piped in her voice singing to the vast crowds. An upset and enraged Nelson stated, "I went straight home and changed my will. When I go, it will be in a private ceremony."

Jeanette's death left Nelson utterly stunned. He couldn't believe she was gone. Above all, her passing brought home to him his own mortality and how good life had been to him.

Sidney and Janine married on November 19, 1965, and the family celebrated with everyone together for Thanksgiving. It was to be the beginning of a happy new life for Sidney as they have now been married for twenty-seven years. But the holidays were overshadowed by gloom. It was hard to celebrate a joyous Christmas as the war in Vietnam escalated forcing our own military to enter the carnage. Another note of sadness was sounded when Walt Disney lost his long battle to cancer.

There was little hope for peace on the horizon as 1966 began. Right after the holidays, Nelson and Gale left for a tightly scheduled tour to the East coast. The weather was terrible. Planes were delayed and blinding blizzards greeted them upon their arrival in New York. Everything that could go wrong did. They were so tired by the time they opened to a packed audience of standing room only at the Latin Quarter, Ted was sure that one of them would collapse from fatigue. By the time they appeared on the "Merv Griffin Show" later in the week, they had gotten some much needed rest and a renewed sense of humor. When Nelson and Gale walked out on stage, Merv quipped, "Ah, there's "The Voice". I have marched with you; I have tramped with you. Now <u>those</u> were movies!" During the show, Merv asked Nelson what his most embarrassing moment was while performing. Nelson grinned, "When I forgot the words to *Shortnin' Bread* in Philadelphia where everyone knows me." Nelson and Gale delighted the audience with a mixture of old and new songs. It was to be Nelson's last television appearance in the United States.

Later that summer, he shared the stage with his dear old friends Edgar Bergen and Guy Lombardo in a special outdoor performance at the Valley Music Hall in San Carlos. It was a reunion of sorts and after the show they visited into the late hours of the morning. Nelson and Guy discussed their upcoming appearance at the Waldorf Astoria. Nelson and Gale were to be guest stars for the annual New Years show.

The holidays gave Nelson a much needed reprieve from work. The whole family gathered at the Eddy's for Christmas dinner. Then it was back to scripts and rehearsals as he and Gale prepared for New York. The televised show at the Waldorf Astoria turned out to be a wonderful evening. Nelson was in perfect form and the show was a smashing success.

Meanwhile the plans in progress for their fourth Australian tour showed all the signs of an oncoming disaster. Nelson became very ill with the flu; Gale had to have minor surgery and Ted wasn't well enough to make the scheduled trip to Australia. All three of them were worn out by the excessive travel, bad weather and many complications which had dogged them of late.

Nelson complained more openly of the constant problems confronting him. He became more combative and his usual humility often spiraled towards self-depreciation.

After a stressful trip, Nelson and Gale opened at Chequers in Sydney, Australia on January 19, 1967 for a three week season. They did two shows, one at 7:00 and one at 11:30. Although this time of year was traditionally slow in Sydney, the crowds were bigger than ever for Nelson's act.

Nelson looked very tired and his deeply lined forehead added even more character. He went straight to the hearts of the people. His voice was as vibrant as ever. This was their best Australian tour and the rewards were evident by the rave reviews and standing room only shows. The "Australian Sun" wrote on January 27, 1967:

> The most durable product of show business "Iron Man Eddy", hit Sydney again last night and he looks like a big hit---again. Nelson Eddy on stage at Chequers sings, "Without a song the day would never end..." From the applause at the beginning, in the middle and at the end of his numbers, it seems Nelson Eddy's day will never end.

Chapter Twenty-Eight

As the warmth of spring unfolded its glories, Nelson, Ted and Gale saw a bright future ahead of them. Well rested and rejuvenated after a short vacation, they were looking forward to this particular tour with special anticipation. After performances at the San Souci in Miami, they would perform at the Civic Opera House in Chicago on March 7th with Nelson's old friend Franklyn MacCormack, then travel on to Canada where Gale had family.

The San Souci was packed for the first performance. Nelson was in perfect voice as he and Gale finished singing several popular favorites. Suddenly, as he poised to sing solo, he had difficulty with the words. Gale vividly recalls that evening.

> I would know if he was sick, had a cold or was down about something. We had just finished *Love and Marriage* where we would each take a different line and would turn our heads to the lights---so to sort of stage it, and this time he didn't respond on his line. Now that was unheard of. I looked at him and he didn't have panic in his eyes, they were just looking. He was detached, different, and a red blotch appeared on the side of his face that wasn't there 10 minutes ago. I sensed something was peculiar but followed our usual routine where I make a costume change while Nelson sings a solo.

To the audience however, Nelson appeared as though his throat had gone dry. Lillian Ranahan was seated about six feet from the stage and when Nelson had difficulty talking, she started to hand a glass of water up to him, but was stopped by her friends. He was holding onto the left side of his face with one hand while holding the microphone in the other.

When Gale neared the stage after her costume change, she heard Nelson say, "Ted, play *Dardinella* and maybe I'll get the words back." Then there was utter silence. Gale continues:

> Even that wasn't so strange, because in the past when Nelson would forget the words to *Shortnin' Bread*, he use to turn and say, "What am I singing? Where am I? Is this Pittsburgh?" But as I walked out to him, I knew there was something terribly wrong. He looked me right in the eye---but there was no recognition.
>
> His face was so blank and he couldn't speak. We asked for a doctor and one came up from the audience as Ted and I got him into a chair off stage. As the doctor examined him, he told us he was either having a stroke or a heart attack.
>
> It seemed forever before an ambulance came. I remember to the best of my knowledge that the money for the ambulance came from that doctor.
>
> Nelson never spoke again, not a word. I tried to think, how am I to do this? Would he approve? At this point I was wearing a white coat, black net stockings and pumps. It was like a bad dream.
>
> The hospital was very busy. There he was lying in his tuxedo with his makeup on. I knew I was in shock ---I just didn't know what to do. I kept thinking---this can't be happening---everything had been going so well.
>
> I wanted desperately to call Ann. But what could I say---I didn't want to call her until I could explain everything to her. So I called my own doctor and he gave me the name of a heart specialist whom I could

> talk to. They took him for tests while I gathered his clothes and carefully folded them.

The doctors diagnosed Nelson as having had a cerebral hemorrhage. They explained to Gale, "There's no way---we don't know how long, but there is certainly no way he'll ever be what he was."

Then Ted arrived with some of Nelson's personal papers. After conferring with Ted, Gale immediately called Ann. Only a few hours had passed. It was still the middle of the night, around 12:00 A.M.

> The doctors had worded everything for me to explain to Ann. My call woke her out of a sound sleep and as I slowly choked out the words, she was beside herself. There she was, nearly seventy and suffering from severe arthritis, all alone with no ticket and no one close to call for help. It's at least a 45 minute drive to the airport. Then Ann talked to the doctor and when he told her that Nelson had only four to six hours to live, if that, she knew she couldn't get there in time---no matter how hard she tried. She was so overcome with sorrow.
>
> "How is he really?" she kept asking.
>
> "Oh Ann, I'm so sorry, so terribly sorry."
>
> "Does he talk?" She tried so hard to be calm, but her voice quivered.
>
> "Ann," I broke down, "Oh dearest, I don't know what to do!"
>
> Ted was overcome by it all. As we sat and waited, I glanced at the clock. It was 3:00 A.M. I talked to Ann. We just talked on and on and when I wasn't talking to Ann, I talked to Nelson and told him everything, just as if he could hear me.
>
> Finally the doctors asked me to leave the room and I felt, if I left, Nelson would leave us forever. Dear

God, it was so hard to walk out of that room. A few minutes later Nelson was gone.

It was dawn as I slowly walked down the corridor and out into the new day. As I walked numbly into the sunlight, I looked up and saw two beautiful white doves soaring off into space. Nelson loved doves and as they flew above me, I said, "There he goes!" I'll never, never see a small white bird and not think of dear Nelson flying away.

Chapter Twenty-Nine

Ann called Sidney, Bill, Marguerite and Ginny right away. It was a terribly difficult task for her, but made easier by the strength and comfort each gave to the other. By mid-morning she had reached everyone but Ginny. That day Ginny was substitute teaching at Nelson's old school, Grove Street Elementary. Whether it be coincidence or divine order, when word finally reached Ginny, although shocked by her sudden grief, she remembers thinking:

> It occurred to me that Nelson was more tangible to me here. For a moment, I closed my eyes and saw a small boy playing the drums in the band and drumming for the children to march in and out at recess.
>
> Rather than go home early, I continued to teach the rest of the day thinking that it would honor Nelson's belief "the show must go on." My own sons attended Grove Street Elementary. It held special memories for all of us. Fifteen years ago it was demolished and replaced by a commercial development.

Bill Eddy had not been well himself so the family's concern had been centered on his well being. To Bill, it was beyond belief that his son would die before him. The pain of his beloved son's passing was almost too much for him to bear. He knew he would be unable to attend the funeral---to him Nelson was still alive.

Gale and Ted had not eaten since 5:00 P.M. the day before and it was now 8:00 in the morning of March 6th. There was nothing more they could do. Gale sadly recalls:

> We sat there with tears rolling down our faces for the longest time. The hotel was wonderful; they helped us with our luggage and transportation so that, after a visit to the mortuary, we were immediately able to board a plane for home. It was daylight when we landed in California. We hadn't slept for two nights. When I saw Ann, my heart just broke; the press was running up to her. Sidney had to push the photographers away. It was such a nightmare.

Sidney angrily recalls, "I didn't want some photographer snapping my mother's picture in her most private moments, so I tried to keep them away until we got her into the car. We went straight to the house."

Gale was in deep shock. "My own mother didn't even know Nelson was gone," Gale sadly explained, "When I told her, I thought she was going to die. She was in her late 70's---the shock of that and oh, how she loved him! We spent the next day at Nelson's house. Ann and I had a long, long cry that day."

Nelson had held firm in his beliefs throughout his life. In death he requested a simple funeral devoid of the media's sensationalism and the public's emotionalism. In keeping with his philosophy, he had chosen Hollywood Memorial Cemetery rather than the luxurious Forest Lawn as a resting place for Isabel, Ann and himself. He wrote in his will, "I believe the body is useless after death. Let there be no sorrow over the remains, for at that time I believe my soul will have found its destined way to the infinite."

March 9th dawned grey and cloudy as family and friends came together to honor him. Although there were television cameras whirling and cameras clicking outside, the scene was devoid of mass hysteria. All was quiet and dignified just as Nelson wanted it.

Their love for this sensitive musical genius was reflected in the actions and expressions of every mourner. Almost all had been friends of Nelson's for many years. Dear friends such as Elinor and Wayne Griffin, Art Rush, his personal manager during the height of his radio days accompanied by his wife Mary Jo; Bobby Armbruster, who had conducted Nelson's "Old Gold" and "Electric Hour" radio shows; Mildred Hudson, his faithful secretary for fifteen years; Harper McKay whose arrangements Nelson had used in his nightclub act; Nelson's cousin Sally Breckner and her husband Bob; and Bob Hunter who had been his musical director on the last Australian tour were among the mourners. They were joined by Doris Kenyon, Ann and Nelson's close friend who had introduced them so very long ago; Thomas Freebarion-Smith, an announcer on many of Nelson's shows; Delmar Davis, Henry Dreyfuss and several members of the Nelson Eddy Music Club.

Ann was accompanied by Gale, Sidney and his wife Janine, their children Victoria, Roxanne, Carol and Elizabeth, Ann's sister Irene May and her family, Ginny, Wayne and Elliott Brown. Ted, Helen and Gale sat with the family in the mourning room out of sight from the others.

The organ played as the pallbearers took their places in the first two pews. They were Gene Raymond, Jeanette's husband, who had flown home from the east coast for the funeral; composer Meredith Willson who had known Nelson long before his movie fame; actor, Lloyd Nolan; his agent, Myron Henly; his doctor, Rex Kemamer; and his business agent, Jim Osborne.

The chapel overflowed with cascades of beautiful flowers shadowed by the soft glow of candles. White carnations blanketed the bronze casket and a large cross of flowers rose immediately above it.

All was quiet as Dr. Jay Herbert Smith of All Saints Episcopal Church in Beverly Hills began the private funeral liturgy. Wayne Griffin gave an emotional eulogy filled with such descriptions as "hilarious clown to sublime artist---a lovable paradox, a simple man yet one of the most delicate, sensitive and complex natures I have ever known." He portrayed Nelson as having been as much a hero to his family and friends as he was to the public.

Ted, who had stood beside Nelson for forty years, remembered him as "one of the world's kindest men". During the memorial service Ted played a song which he had written for Nelson, *Der Tod das ist die kuhle Nacht,*---"Death is the Cool Night". After the services at the cemetery, family and friends returned to Nelson's home. Gale recalls how kind and helpful everyone was.

> I remember Gene Raymond came over and asked, "How are you doing?" He was so nice to me. I don't know if I had ever met him before, but it was so good of him.
>
> "I don't know, Gene," I said, "I hope I've done right."
>
> He patted and assured me, "It was fine."
>
> Then the reality set in. I didn't see Ann for awhile, but we talked every other day on the phone.
>
> Ann always knew what she had to go through. Her faith was tremendous. It supported her through a house to sell, papers to go through, a lifetime of love for Nelson. She was very respectful of what others thought. She responded to the fans and the memorials. Such a hard chore, but one that you have to do alone. Ann saw it all through with grace and style.

Sidney recalls Ann telling him many times over, "Nelson honored the faith of those who had held him in fond esteem and I am eternally grateful that he never knew the bitterness of failure in his profession."

After the funeral, Thelma had the difficult task of disbanding The Nelson Eddy Music Club.

> I can't begin to remember all the phone calls, letters, and notes we received, but I remember how shocked and saddened everyone was. I spoke with Gale first, then Ann and later with Mildred Hudson. I kept remembering that I was going to disappoint his fans by disbanding the club but this was Nelson's wish.

Thelma published one last issue of the "Shooting Star". It was a memorial issue in which Nelson's family and friends contributed letters of tribute and memories. Dad Eddy evoked everyone's feelings when he wrote, "It came so suddenly, it's so hard to believe, even today he seems to be alive." Some of Nelson's friends who contributed to the memorial journal were Lloyd Nolan, Dennis O'Keefe, Eleanor Powell, Robert Merrill, Greer Garson, Gene Raymond, Bob Hope, Joan Crawford, and Peter Lind-Hayes.

Ann was overwhelmed by the burden before her. Through scalding tears of sorrow, she and she alone spent hours going through Nelson's personal mementos, art work and music library. She cautiously shielded his personal belongings from the fans and general public. At times she became white with anger at the behavior of the fans. Sidney remembers, "After Nelson's death, people would go through her garbage." Ann chose to burn whatever she could not give to family or friends rather than have them fall into the wrong hands.

She held on tightly to their dear friends, Doris Kenyon and Elinor and Wayne Griffin. Many nights she called them for counsel, wanting to be sure to do the right thing.

Thelma agrees that Ann's strongest desire was to honor Nelson's memory.

> Ann always kept in touch after Nelson's passing. She would phone often. She never cut herself off from us or the few other fans she knew and trusted. Mildred Hudson remained her secretary and dear friend until Millie's own untimely death. My friendship with Ann continued throughout the years and she continually amazed me because of her constant love and remembrances of Nelson. She often gave anonymous gifts in his memory.

Gene Raymond married ten years after Jeanette's passing, but for Ann, that was not to be. Gale remembers quite clearly just how adamant she was on the subject. One night she called Gale complaining, "My friends invited this widowed gentleman to dinner suggesting he would be a nice companion for me, and I told them very firmly that no man could ever come close to Nelson." She chose to live in Nelson's memory for twenty years until her death.

Gale was reeling from her loss as well. Her life was now painfully altered forever.

> I stood beside him for fifteen years. I had no agent, no plans, there was nothing for me. In the beginning I would go to his grave site every day.
>
> Two months after Nelson's passing, Edwin Lester of the Los Angeles Civic Light Opera called and asked me to audition for "Showboat". He asked me to sing *Bill* which was a very dramatic song.
>
> On the night of my first performance the song came across beautifully because my emotions were right on the surface. Had Nelson been there, he would have said, "Well done." Liberace saw that performance and offered me a job.

Living in Nelson's memory wasn't always easy for Gale. Even after working with Liberace for a year, she was still introduced as Nelson Eddy's singing partner. But at 38, she was back on her feet and making it alone.

> I believe Nelson guided me through all those times of independence and growth. I was able to handle the problems of being on the road because of Nelson's astute training. I kept in touch with Ann often, always letting her know how I was doing.
>
> I returned to Australia one more time and performed in front of 5,000 people. They were wonderful and gave me a standing ovation. My last performance there meant a great deal to me. I'll cherish the memories of their kindness forever.

Ted felt adrift in his own sorrow. He and Nelson had been inseparable for so many years. Neither had ever thought about an ending. After talking at length with Helen and the boys, Ted decided to teach music at Pasadena University.

To his legions of fans, as well as those who had known him well, there is no requiem for Nelson. He walked among us honestly, lovingly and unpretentiously, then his spirit winged away just as he had wanted it to...in the middle of a song. He left us a legacy in his art and music, his bountiful zest for life and his gracious, merry nature. For all whose lives were touched by him---his song goes on forever.

EPILOGUE

A year after Nelson's death, Ann donated his extensive collection of scores, oratories and music to the Occidental College Music Library in Los Angeles, California. On November 3, 1968, Bill Eddy passed away. The family, still reeling from Nelson's death, felt their loss deeply. Ann found solace in her family and friends. She knew who was a fan, a trusted friend or a busybody. She helped Doris and Elinor handle the burden and sorrow of their own husbands' passing. Every Sunday she drove to Nelson's grave, and when she was confined to a wheelchair because of her worsening condition, someone else drove her. But always, she visited Nelson.

Whenever Sidney and Janine expressed concern because she was living alone, Ann remained adamant. "I don't need anyone. I have Nelson," she'd affirm. In later years, she finally acquiesced, but the nurses were always referred to as housekeepers by the family.

Gale performed with Liberace for a year and then joined the "Arthur Godfrey Show". She also continued to perform light opera. While returning from a trip to Barbados in 1975, Gale met Charles Francis, the Captain of her Eastern Airlines flight. After a short time, both of them felt as though they had known each other all their lives. Three months later, Gale took Charles to meet Ann. Charles knew he had passed the muster when Ann queried, "Gale dear, when is the marriage to take place?" They joyously granted her wish several weeks later and have been happily married for seventeen years.

Ted retired from teaching because of his failing health. He passed away on September 16, 1979.

In 1984, David Wolper asked Ann Eddy if she would agree to a two-part series on Nelson. Ann had tried so often to set the record straight in the past. She didn't feel strong enough to try again.

The years had taken their toll on her health and she was tired. On August 28, 1987, six weeks before her 93rd birthday, Ann passed away. Next to her bed, Sidney and Janine found a small silver box. Inside was a note written in brush strokes by Nelson. It read: "I will love you forever and ever."

MOVIES OF NELSON EDDY

1933	***DANCING LADY*** METRO-GOLDEN-MAYER JOAN CRAWFORD, CLARK GABLE, FRANCHOT TONE
1934	***BROADWAY TO HOLLYWOOD*** METRO-GOLDEN-MAYER ALICE BRADY, FRANK MORGAN
1934	***STUDENT TOUR*** METRO-GOLDEN-MAYER JIMMY DURANTE, CHARLES BUTTERWORTH, MAXINE DOYLE, PHIL REGAN
1935	***NAUGHTY MARIETTA*** METRO-GOLDEN-MAYER JEANETTE MACDONALD, NELSON EDDY, FRANK MORGAN, ELSA LANCHESTER
1936	***ROSEMARIE*** METRO-GOLDEN-MAYER JEANETTE MACDONALD, NELSON EDDY,
1937	***MAYTIME*** METRO-GOLDEN-MAYER JEANETTE MACDONALD, NELSON EDDY, JOHN BARRYMORE
1937	***ROSALIE*** METRO-GOLDEN-MAYER NELSON EDDY, ELEANOR POWELL, ILONA MASSEY

1938 ***GIRL OF THE GOLDEN WEST***
METRO-GOLDEN-MAYER
JEANETTE MACDONALD, NELSON EDDY

1938 ***SWEETHEARTS***
METRO-GOLDEN-MAYER
JEANETTE MACDONALD, NELSON EDDY

1939 ***LET FREEDOM RING***
METRO-GOLDEN-MAYER
NELSON EDDY, VIRGINIA BRUCE

1939 ***BALALAIKA***
METRO-GOLDEN-MAYER
NELSON EDDY, ILONA MASSEY

1940 ***NEW MOON***
METRO-GOLDEN-MAYER
JEANETTE MACDONALD, NELSON EDDY

1940 ***BITTERSWEET***
METRO-GOLDEN-MAYER
JEANETTE MACDONALD, NELSON EDDY

1941 ***THE CHOCOLATE SOLDIER***
METRO-GOLDEN-MAYER
NELSON EDDY, RISE STEVENS,
NIGEL BRUCE

1942 ***I MARRIED AN ANGEL***
METRO-GOLDEN-MAYER
JEANETTE MACDONALD, NELSON EDDY

1943 ***THE PHANTOM OF THE OPERA***
UNIVERSAL
NELSON EDDY, SUSANNA FOSTER,
CLAUDE RAINS

1944 ***KNICKERBOCKER HOLIDAY***
METRO-GOLDEN-MAYER
NELSON EDDY, CHARLES COBURN,
CONSTANCE DOWLING

1946 ***MAKE MINE MUSIC***
WALT DISNEY - RKO
NELSON EDDY, BENNY GOODMAN,
DINAH SHORE, THE ANDREW SISTERS

1947 ***NORTHWEST OUTPOST***
REPUBLIC
NELSON EDDY, ILONA MASSEY